Fortress Scotland

Militarism, State and Society

Series editor: Dan Smith

Pluto's series on militarism, state and society provides political analysis as well as new information and argument relating to current political controversies in the field of nuclear weapons, military policy and disarmament. It aims to present radical analyses and critiques of the existing orthodoxies in readable and accessible form.

Malcolm Spaven

Fortress Scotland

A guide to the military presence

Pluto Press
in association with Scottish CND

First published in 1983 by Pluto Press Limited,
The Works, 105a Torriano Avenue, London NW5 2RX
and Pluto Press Australia Limited, PO Box 199, Leichhardt
New South Wales 2040, Australia

Set by Alan Sutton Publishing Limited
17a Brunswick Road, Gloucester

Printed in Great Britain by
Garden City Press, Letchworth, Herts

British Library Cataloguing in Publication Data
Spaven, Malcolm
    Fortress Scotland: a guide to the military presence.
    1. Scotland—Military history
    2. Scotland—History
    I. Title
    355′009411   DA767

ISBN 0 86104 735 4

Contents

Foreword by Scottish CND

In 1983 more and more people in Britain demand the right to know what the government is doing in their name, and with their money, in the field of military spending. Defence is now at the centre of political debate in this country, and governments are no longer in a position to push ahead with multi-billion pound defence spending programmes in secrecy as they did with the Polaris Chevaline programme.

The peace movement now has a vital role to play in the debate on Britain's military posture, not merely in ridding the country of nuclear weapons, but increasingly in shaping a truly defensive, non-nuclear defence policy. To do so, however, the peace movement, and the public in general, must know something about the activities of the armed forces in their local area, and how these fit into the wider context of NATO policy and the manoeuvring of the superpowers. This is particularly the case with the move towards a 'first strike' capability, of which Britain's Trident D5 is part. Britain's new 'deterrent', Trident, is a massive unilateral increase in nuclear weaponry, and will be added to the 23,000 new nuclear warheads which the Americans alone plan to produce through the 1980s.

While the Falklands war has led to a desire by some for Britain to regain its imperial role of gunboat diplomacy in the Third World, there are also major implications for Britain's role in NATO. In Scotland, with the concentration of strategic missile submarines in the Clyde, and a plethora of bases associated with anti-submarine warfare and the command and control of maritime forces in the North Atlantic, the Falklands experience is likely to lead to further military expansion as the ability to fight a war in, over, and under the Atlantic Ocean receives more emphasis. The aim of this book is to set out the context in which these Scottish bases operate, the nuclearisation of the North Atlantic, the trends towards a war-fighting strategy, and the impact of military activity on Scotland. It is hoped that this will both contribute to public knowledge of the role of the military in Scotland, and assist campaigners in opposing nuclear weapons and military expansionism. Campaigning along with other North Atlantic countries is a possible follow-up from the book, for example the Nuclear Free North Atlantic conference of April 1983. The worrying developments at Stornoway are of immediate concern.

Scottish CND hope that this book will stimulate further research and that this will lead to a regular exchange of information, updating of the book and keeping abreast of military developments. There are many areas not covered in this publication – for example, civil defence, which has received a great deal of attention in other publications.

The campaign against nuclear weapons in Scotland has taken on a new lease of life since the general election of 1983. Campaigners can see a massive increase in the nuclear arsenals, and although recognising a change of political pace is required in campaigning against them, they are not giving up, but forming new groups, new alliances. Many campaigners in Scotland now see the need to work through stages – such as the 'freeze' and a 'no first use' agreement. This is not to weaken or replace SCND's commitment to unilateral nuclear disarmament, but to mobilise the majority opinion opposed to cruise and Trident and draw it into action.

Scottish CND, and the author, would welcome any amendments, corrections or additions to this book.

Neil McKechnie
General Secretary, Scottish CND

Preface and acknowledgements

Britain's long traditions of government secrecy make it difficult to obtain detailed information on the activities of the military. Most books on the subject focus on the ceremonial, historical and glamorous aspects of the armed forces at the expense of explaining what exactly the military does, and why. For this reason it is necessary to make use of myriad sources available to the public in order to build up a picture of local and regional military presence which can then be related to what is known about defence policy and strategy.

A surprisingly detailed picture of the military can be built up merely by visiting a local library. Telephone directories list the main installations, while the local authority valuation rolls list all property owned or leased by the MOD. Local authority planning registers provide details of building and other developments at military sites in the area, while a regular scanning of the local, regional and national press is extremely important for research of this kind. Above all, informed observation can add flesh to the bare bones of published data on the military.

There are many specialist journals on defence. These are not, unfortunately, widely available, but can be obtained with perseverance. Also of use are the military's in-house journals, such as RAF News, Navy News and Soldier. These can be obtained from military careers offices or public libraries. Finally, it is a sad irony that more can often be learned about military activities in the UK from American government sources than from British. In this respect, the published hearings of US congressional committees provide a wealth of information, although they are difficult to obtain in Britain.

Acknowledgements are due to many people for their help in

writing this book. First, the book was co-written with Keith Bryers, whose extensive knowledge and painstaking research made the whole project possible. Sincere thanks are also due to everyone at ADIU, Billie Bielckus, Duncan Campbell, Paul Claesson, Rob Edwards, all at Glasgow END, Nils Peter Gleditsch, and Keep NATO Out Committee, Donnie and Fiona Macdonald, Rory Macdonald, Robert Moore, Scottish CND, Jon Side and TAG(s), Dan Smith, Owen Wilkes, Evan Wylie and the considerable number of people who supplied snippets of information which all assisted in building up an overall view of the military presence in Scotland.

Abbreviations

ASW	anti-submarine warfare
AWACS	Airborne Warning and Control System (the USAF/NATO Boeing E-3 aircraft)
BAOR	British Army of the Rhine
BMEWS	Ballistic Missile Early Warning System
BNFL	British Nuclear Fuels Ltd
BT	British Telecom
BUTEC	British Underwater Test and Evaluation Centre
C^3I	command, control, communications and intelligence
DCN	Defence Communications Network (British)
DF	(radio) direction finding
DSCS	Defense Satellite Communications System (American)
FLTSATCOM	Fleet Satellite Communications (US navy)
FOSIC	Fleet Ocean Surveillance Information Center (US navy)
GCHQ	Government Communications Headquarters
HF	high frequency radio
IFF	identification friend or foe
LF	low frequency radio
MIRV	multiple independently targetable re-entry vehicles (several nuclear warheads on one missile)
MOD	Ministry of Defence
MOD(PE)	Ministry of Defence Procurement Executive
NADGE	NATO Air Defence Ground Environment
NATO	North Atlantic Treaty Organisation

NATS	National Air Traffic Services
NDB	nuclear depth bomb
NERC	Natural Environment Research Council
NIP	NATO Infrastructure Programme
NSA	National Security Agency (American)
OSIS	Ocean Surveillance Information System (US navy)
OTC	Officer Training Corps
POL	petroleum, oil and lubricants
RAF	Royal Air Force
RAMC	Royal Army Medical Corps
RAOC	Royal Army Ordnance Corps
R AUX AF	Royal Auxiliary Air Force
RCT	Royal Corps of Transport
RE	Royal Engineers
REME	Royal Electrical and Mechanical Engineers
RFA	Royal Fleet Auxiliary
RMAS	Royal Maritime Auxiliary Service
RMC	Royal Marine Commando
RMP	Royal Military Police
RN	Royal Navy
RNR	Royal Naval Reserve
ROC	Royal Observer Corps
SACEUR	NATO's Supreme Allied Commander Europe
SACLANT	NATO's Supreme Allied Commander Atlantic
SAS	Special Air Service
SBS	Special Boat Squadron
SCATCC	Scottish Air Traffic Control Centre, Prestwick
SDD	Scottish Development Department
SHF	super high frequency radio
SHHD	Scottish Home and Health Department (responsible for civil defence in Scotland)
SIGINT	signals intelligence
SOSUS	sound surveillance system
SSN	nuclear-powered ballistic missile submarine
SSBN	nuclear-powered attack submarine or 'hunter-killer'

STCICS	Strike Command Integrated Communications System (run by the RAF)
TARE	Telecommunications Automatic Relay Equipment (part of the NATO Integrated Communications System)
TASS	Telecommunications Automatic Switching System (part of the NATO Integrated Communications System)
TAVR	Territorial and Army Volunteer Reserve
UHF	ultra high frequency radio
UKADGE	United Kingdom Air Defence Ground Environment
UKAEA	United Kingdom Atomic Energy Authority
UKMS	United Kingdom Microwave System (US navy)
UKWMO	United Kingdom Atomic Energy Authority Organisation
USAF	United States Air Force
USMC	United States Marine Corps
USN	United States Navy
(v)	Volunteer (signifying a TAVR unit)
VHF	very high frequency radio
VLF	very low frequency radio
WRAC	Women's Royal Army Corps

1. The strategists' Scotland

Scotland is usually seen as being a peripheral country, stuck out on the north-west fringes of Europe. To the military planners things look rather different. Scotland sits in a commanding position overlooking the vast expanses of the north-east Atlantic. It lies on the shortest routes by air, sea and telecommunications from the USA to Europe, and it has large expanses of sparsely populated terrain suitable for military training.

These geographical factors have combined with political circumstances since 1945 to place Scotland at the centre of superpower and military bloc rivalries. The USA has for many years sought to prevent any conflict, even world war, infringing on its own territory. This requires a 'forward defence' strategy – a vast network of foreign military bases in some 45 countries around the world from which the USA can exert its military and political power.[1] Current trends under Reagan are stressing the global 'power projection' capabilities and goals of the US military, notably in the form of the Rapid Deployment Joint Task Force (RDJTF), which is designed primarily for intervention in the Persian Gulf, and the unprecedented expansion of the US navy towards a goal of global maritime superiority.

At the same time the $180 billion expansion of US strategic nuclear forces under Reagan, announced in 1981, not only puts the arms race into a new phase of acceleration but sucks even more countries around the world into the system of threat and counter-threat which is at the heart of the military bloc system. Deployment and patrol areas for the new generation of air, sea and land-based cruise missiles, communications stations for the transmission of launch orders, reconnaissance and surveillance facilities to provide data for the targeting of nuclear weapons, and navigation systems to ensure the accuracy of nuclear strikes must be located right across the globe if the USA is to achieve its stated aim of being able to fight a global nuclear war and 'prevail' at the end of it.

In this sense the military confrontation between the USA and the USSR is not merely a question of fields of missile silos, fleets of submarines and aircraft posturing at each other across the 'Iron Curtain'. It is a highly complex network of facilities throughout the world which in turn entails a web of political and military relationships between the superpowers and their 'host' countries. These relationships are essential to the continued dominance of the USA and the USSR in world affairs. Their importance makes it extremely difficult for any nation regarded as vital to the interests of either military bloc to achieve or sustain true independence, non-alignment or neutrality.

For the USSR, the maintenance of its international political and military status rests heavily on its East European satellite states. Its attempts to establish and consolidate Soviet influence in other parts of the world – China, Angola, Afghanistan – have created more problems than the Kremlin would have wished. For the USA, the extension of political and military power abroad since 1945 has always had behind it the power of the dollar. Nations involved in politico-military relationships with the USA know that there is always the prospect, for some at least, of crumbs from the rich man's table. This makes America's grip on other countries much firmer and more dependable – though by no means guaranteed, as Vietnam, Nicaragua and Iran have shown.

Scotland is a part of this international web of US military presence overseas. However, it is not only sucked into the Cold War through its status as a client of the Pentagon. Its position as an integral part of the second biggest member of NATO in military terms, and on the edge of a strategically vital ocean area for the superpowers, gives Scotland a political and military status in NATO out of all proportion to its size. This is not a simple accident of geography. The Soviet decision to concentrate its strategic submarine fleet in the Kola Peninsula, the American stress on submarine and anti-submarine technology, on cruise missile deployment in the north-east Atlantic, and on the need to send a million troops to Europe in wartime – all these are *political* decisions, in which considerations of strategy, technology, economics and politics interact with the simple dictates of geography. In a world free of superpower posturing, the north-east Atlantic might have increased economic and resource importance, but its military functions would be almost entirely eclipsed. Scotland's role as a part of NATO mortgages its own security to the conflicting national interests of the USA and the USSR.

A third factor shaping the nature, number and role of military installations in Scotland is its contribution to the armed forces of the UK. This also affects the use made of Scotland for military training and operations and the way in which 'defence' is perceived in Scotland.

There is a long tradition in Scotland of providing recruits for the armed forces and merchant marine of the UK, predominantly for the lower ranks of the 'poor bloody infantry'. This tradition endures, with Scotland currently providing 7 out of the British army's total of 37 infantry regiments. The MOD does not publish figures on the geographical distribution of service recruitment, but with consistently high unemployment in Scotland and concentrated recruiting drives in certain areas, the Scottish contribution of military personnel per head of population is likely to be higher than the UK average.

The current government shows no signs of accepting that the UK's retention of a global military intervention capability and an 'independent' strategic nuclear force are an expensive and dangerous anachronism. Scotland provides both a base and a refit facility for the UK strategic nuclear force, and important training facilities for land, sea and air forces whose roles have very little to do with the defence of Britain. Similarly, the US presence in Scotland – strategic nuclear submarines, communications links, anti-submarine weapon stocks, electronic and signals intelligence bases – places Scotland firmly in a global context as an integral element of the USA's 'forward defence' of its own national interests.

Functions of the military presence

Scotland's military installations cannot be seen in isolation. They are an illustration, on a local scale, of the myriad facilities required to support international military confrontation. Scotland hosts military activities in all three areas of operations, training, and research and development. Although outside the scope of this book, there is also a large Scottish military industrial base, with Marconi, Ferranti and Yarrows amongst the biggest weapons contractors to the MOD and foreign governments. Scottish universities also play their part in military-funded research for the MOD and the Pentagon.

Scottish bases perform a variety of roles within the three broad categories of general military preparations, facilities related to nuclear weapons, and research, development, production and testing of weapons.

General military preparations range from the training of infantry recruits, which has been established as one of the Scottish military specialisms, through equipment repair facilities as at Almondbank and Forthside, to flying training and operations from the three main RAF airfields at Leuchars, Kinloss and Lossiemouth. Many of these activities might constitute sensible elements of a non-nuclear defence policy. The fishery protection and oil-rig surveillance patrols by the RN from Rosyth, and perhaps some aspects of the air defence activities at Leuchars, are the sort of functions which could have a 'non-offensive' character.[2] However, under present conditions even infantry and TAVR training activities contribute substantially to preparations for nuclear war in Europe, for military intervention outside the NATO area, and for 'home defence', i.e. the suppression of internal dissent in the run-up to war.[3]

Scotland has a heavy concentration of military installations connected with nuclear weapons. Holy Loch and Coulport together may hold as many as 1,700 warheads for Poseidon and Polaris missiles at any one time, while Machrihanish holds stocks of air-delivered nuclear depth bombs. Chapelcross produces tritium and plutonium for Britain's bombs, while Dounreay and Rosyth are responsible for developing and maintaining the propulsion systems of Britain's nuclear submarines. Training of nuclear forces is carried out at South Uist (where practice firings of the army's Lance missile are conducted) and throughout the vast low-flying areas where strike aircraft practise nuclear bombing missions. Command, control, communications and intelligence (c^3i) facilities for nuclear forces exist at a number of installations, notably Forss/West Murkle, Mormond Hill, Edzell, Scatsta and Pitreavie, while the UK Warning and Monitoring Organisation (UKWMO) network in Scotland provides the attack warning and assessment information necessary to conduct a nuclear war.

Research, development, production and testing of all manner of weaponry is a prominent aspect of the Scottish military presence. Air-delivered weapons trials are carried out at West Freugh, armoured vehicle weapons at Dundrennan, and underwater weapons in the Sound of Raasay and all but one of the sea lochs in the Clyde. Other research facilities in Scotland are responsible for ship structures, sonar, radio propagation and gun propellants.

Although Scotland's military presence is a varied one, there are three areas in which Scotland plays a special role in war preparations: the US reinforcement of Europe before and during war, anti-submarine warfare operations, and c^3i installations. These are discussed below in the context of NATO strategy.

Scotland, NATO and the North Atlantic

Scotland's role in NATO is closely linked to the perceived military functions of the north-east Atlantic and the Norwegian and Barents Seas – known collectively as 'Northern Waters'. The Royal Navy contributes about 70 per cent of NATO's naval forces in this and the Channel Command areas, with the US navy's strong nuclear submarine and aircraft carrier forces making up much of the rest. In general, NATO has considerable military superiority over the Warsaw Pact forces in this area, a fact which has been openly stated by senior US and British government ministers.[4]

This area and its littoral have always been important to the military in the event of a Central European conflict. It would be a haven in their plans to opt for escalation to the use of nuclear weapons, the idea being that SLBMs would be held here in readiness. This still applies, but there is now a movement towards seeing the area as an arena of armed conflict rather than a haven prior to escalation.

The 'strategic' and 'tactical' missions and capabilities of military forces interact in the Northern Waters perhaps more than anywhere else. The 'strategic' dimension lies in the USSR basing and holding ready most of its 'retaliatory' SSBN (nuclear-powered ballistic missile-carrying submarine) force here and also in NATO's requirement to eliminate that force by strategic anti-submarine warfare (SASW). The area is 'tactically' important to the superpowers firstly because of the USSR's likely attempt to move its 'tactical' naval forces (especially diesel and nuclear attack submarines) and aircraft through NATO barriers (e.g. between Greenland and Scotland) to attack sea and airborne reinforcements and crucial coastal areas; secondly because of NATO's efforts to counter these Soviet moves; and thirdly because of NATO offensive actions into the area.

The latter are now a central plank of US naval policy, while the shift of emphasis in British maritime forces from surface ships to submarines and patrol aircraft mirrors the US policy lead. In his report to Congress for the fiscal year 1983, US Navy Secretary John Lehman emphasised that the USA 'must have a forward strategy, a strategy which identifies and exploits Soviet weaknesses such as inherently unfavourable maritime geography', with the aim of 'keeping the Soviets concerned with threats all around their periphery'. 'This strategy requires a force equipped and trained for flexibility, mobility, simultaneity and offensive combat'.[5] This strategy of 'forward deployment' of offensive forces, such as nuclear-armed carrier-borne aircraft and cruise missile-armed ships and submarines, is designed to 'bottle up' the Soviet Northern Fleet in port and form 'choke-points' and 'barriers' in certain key ocean areas through which Soviet naval forces must make passage in war. Such areas include the Barents and Norwegian Seas and the Greenland–

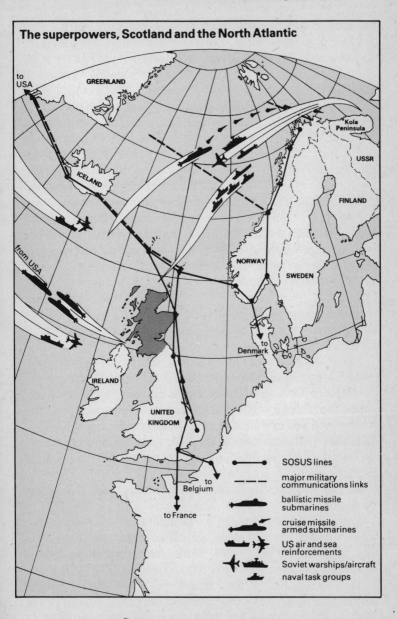

The superpowers, Scotland and the North Atlantic

GREENLAND

to USA

Kola Peninsula

USSR

ICELAND

FINLAND

from USA

NORWAY

SWEDEN

to Denmark

IRELAND

UNITED KINGDOM

to Belgium

to France

● — ● SOSUS lines

– – – major military communications links

ballistic missile submarines

cruise missile armed submarines

US air and sea reinforcements

Soviet warships/aircraft

naval task groups

Iceland–UK gap (usually referred to as the GIUK gap).

Lehman is on record as saying that 'the situation in the North Atlantic and the North Sea clearly favours NATO. There is no question in my mind that we could hold the entire NATO north flank and protect Norway and Denmark'. This would involve the adoption of 'a forward defensive position in Norway that could neutralise the military complex in the Kola Peninsula'.[6] No doubt the latter action would involve nuclear weapons of the US fleet. MccGwire has pointed out that both the main VMF (Soviet navy) SSBN/SSN bases – Petropavlosk-Kamchatka for the Pacific Fleet, and Polyarnyy for the Northern Fleet – are 'at the extremities of the land, remote from centres of population [though more than a million people live around Polyarnyy] and hence suitable targets for surgical nuclear strikes'.[7] MccGwire has also suggested that bases in the north of Scotland could be used for ground-launched cruise missiles targeted on this area, while the former Commander-in-Chief of Allied Forces Northern Europe (CINCAFNORTH), General Sir Peter Whiteley, is on record as saying he believed nuclear weapons could be used to stop a Soviet advance in north Norway without much fear of escalation.[8]

The Soviet Northern Fleet has in any case a number of severe disadvantages in operating from the Kola bases. These are the only Soviet ports which are ice-free all year round, yet their access to the open ocean is restricted by 'choke-points' off the North Cape and in the GIUK gap. The concentration of the SSBN and other submarine fleets in the Kola area and their operational limitations has meant that a large percentage of these vessels lie in the open, unprotected, at Kola at any one time. This may make the 'surgical strike', with all its consequences, a tempting US option.

There is already concern in Scandinavia as to where the various trends towards increased militarisation and confrontation in the north may lead. Some consider that the Soviet concentration around Kola is not incommensurate with legitimate Soviet interests and should be viewed in its global perspective. Even pro-NATO commentators have warned of the dangers of an ill-conceived build-up in the north inconsistent with existing political restraints in the area and which might give the USSR incentive for 'some nervous adventure in the north'.[9] Evidently such fears are not shared by the Pentagon.

In fact the credibility of several basic tenets of NATO policy is seriously threatened when war on the Northern Flank or in Northern Waters is discussed. Caspar Weinberger stated in his report to Congress in 1983 that 'our sea-based nuclear forces for land attack . . . support our policy objective of denying the Soviets the ability to limit a nuclear war to the sea'.[10] However, it was revealed in recently declassified Pentagon documents that the commanders of US navy ships, equipped since the 1950s with the Talos and Terrier nuclear anti-aircraft missile systems, have the authority to release those weapons without the specific presidential authority required for nuclear weapons release in other cases.[11] This means that either the USA thinks it can keep a nuclear war limited to the sea after first use by a harassed US navy captain, or it is prepared to accept, and match, the likely Soviet nuclear response.

As the quotations above show, there are also strongly held views within the military establishment that the Northern Flank is a suitable place for conducting a limited nuclear war on land and/or at sea. This view, if it was ever credible, has now been demolished by the deployment of sea-launched cruise missiles (SLCMS) on US navy ships and submarines. Nuclear powered attack submarines (SSNS) armed with these weapons would form the spearhead of the projected 'surgical strikes' on the Kola bases in the early stages of war. However, although they might be firing conventionally-armed cruise missiles, the USSR has no way of telling nuclear and conventional SLCMS from each other, so would be likely to launch their nuclear response as soon as any cruise missile was detected heading for Kola. Since the USSR's ASW capability is meagre in comparison with the West's, it would not waste time looking for the SSNS firing the cruise missiles; direct strikes would be made on land targets, notably those in the UK, Iceland and Norway associated with the command and control of naval forces in Northern Waters.[12]

It is continually drummed into the minds of the European public that NATO is a purely defensive alliance. The USA's openly aggressive posturing in Northern Waters is leading to doubts about this in many circles, not least in Scandinavia.

Scotland, with its array of reception facilities for US reinforcements, ASW bases, communications stations, SSBN facilities, naval weapons stocks and fuel depots, provides a vital launching point and support base for these activities in Northern Waters.

Anti-submarine warfare and 'limited nuclear war'

The notion that nuclear deterrence works and is stable depends to a great extent on the existence on both sides of a secure retaliatory deterrent which cannnot be knocked out in a first strike. The nuclear ballistic missile submarine (SSBN) is the only weapon that fits this bill. The US has 60 per cent, the USSR only 30 per cent, of their strategic nuclear warheads on SSBNS.

In the past it has been assumed that the task of locating and destroying all enemy SSBNs would be impossible. However, there are indications that generous funding and successive technical advances in ASW techniques may soon give the USA the capability to track and destroy every Soviet SSBN in a first strike.

Until recently, all US declarations about ASW have stressed that US efforts are 'tactical' in nature, i.e. directed not against SSBNS but against Soviet attack submarines.[13] In fact the USA has for many years been developing an anti-SSBN capability, and in May 1983 it was admitted by the US Chief of Naval Operations that US SSNS had increased their under-ice training with the aim of countering any attempt by the USSR to use Arctic waters as a haven or bastion for SSBN operations.[14]

While US ASW capabilities are highly developed, those of the USSR are limited. A senior MOD official stated in 1980 that 'even with Polaris the Soviet navy has never in fact found one of our submarines on patrol',[15] while the US navy remains confident that 'our SLBM [submarine-launched ballistic missile] force is neither at risk today nor in any sense for the foreseeable future.'[16] This marked Western superiority in an area crucial to the security of Soviet retaliatory capability is potentially very destabilising.

Scotland contributes in several ways to US/NATO ASW efforts, mainly because it is a suitable 'host' country at the southern end of the GIUK gap.

The hub of Western ASW is the network of US undersea surveillance systems. These were first deployed in the mid-1950s, with hydrophone arrays known as CAESAR off the east coast of the USA. Shortly afterwards, experimental systems were installed in the Sea of Japan and, apparently, off Shetland. By 1974 the USA had 22 shore stations around the world for its SOSUS (Sound Surveillance System) network, including installations in Iceland, Norway, the UK, Denmark and Canada. Massive investment in research into underwater sound propagation has steadily improved SOSUS capabilities. It has been stated that the system can detect submarines over 1,100 miles away, and localise them to an area as small as 10 miles in diameter.[17]

From all the published evidence it appears that SOSUS, with the exception of a partly NATO-financed installation off the Azores, is wholly US funded. Shore stations within the NATO area are believed to exist under bilateral agreements between the USA and 'host' governments, and are not NATO facilities. This contention is strengthened by the fact that SOSUS is very firmly tied into the Worldwide Military Command and Control System (WWMMCS) which the Pentagon requires to control its nuclear forces. It is believed that in the case of Norway, which does not permit foreign troops to be permanently based on its soil in peacetime, the ocean surveillance facilities are operated by the Norwegian navy but that the USA decides the tasks and location and pays the bill. Such arrangements may exist elsewhere within NATO.

SOSUS and other ocean surveillance data is probably supplied to NATO at the discretion of the USA. The US navy has a major Fleet Ocean Surveillance Centre (FOSIC) at its European HQ in a bunker at Northwood, London, which may decide on the allocation of surveillance and other intelligence data to NATO for use at Pitreavie command centre and elsewhere.

Parallel with developments in acoustic detection, the USA has integrated its undersea sensors with highly advanced data relay and processing facilities. This now enables the US navy not only to track all submarines globally in 'real time', but to integrate the command and control of tracking operations and provide data very rapidly to ASW commanders on ships, aircraft and submarines. This is known as the Integrated Undersea Surveillance System (IUSS). It includes SOSUS and a number of other submarine detection systems: Tactical Towed Array Sonar (TACTAS), deployed on ASW-assigned warships; Surveillance Towed Array Sensor System (SURTASS), which is being deployed on vessels specially built for the purpose of open-ocean surveillance; and the Rapidly Deployable Surveillance System (RDSS), which consists of a torpedo-shaped seabed sonar buoy which can be laid by aircraft, ships or submarines 'in priority areas during crises or conflict.'[18] Compressed bursts of data are transmitted from these to satellites or aircraft.

Satellites are also a vital part of the US ASW programme, providing meteorological and oceanographic information, communications and data relay. Edzell's function of controlling and receiving data from ocean surveillance satellites is an important contribution. The USA is also investigating the possibility of detecting submarines from satellites.[19]

The cost of mounting a programme on this scale is enormous. In 1982 the USA spent $6,000 million on tracking submarines.

Asw weapons are also an important feature of the Scottish contribution to US/NATO superiority in this area. This includes bases for submarines, ships, aircraft and helicopters and stockpiles of conventional and nuclear ASW weapons.

The long-range maritime patrol aircraft (LRMPA), such as the British Nimrod or US/NATO P-3 Orion, is perhaps the most flexible ASW weapon for both strategic surveillance in peacetime and as a 'counter-force' weapon against nuclear submarines in war. The 'tactical' and 'strategic' aspects of ASW become very blurred in relation to LRMPAS as both roles are performed by the same aircraft and use similar systems.

There are three assigned bases for LRMPAS in Scotland – Kinloss, Machrihanish and Stornoway.

The most effective use of US/NATO LRMPAS is in response to intelligence derived from surveillance sensors such as SOSUS. The need for speed and accuracy in response to contact data, so that SSBNs could be destroyed before launching their missiles, emphasises the military importance of effective systems for command, control, communications and intelligence (C^3I) (see *Milltown, Crimond* in chapter 4). Fast secure dissemination of intelligence on surveillance contacts enables an LRMPA to make a direct transit flight to a well-defined target area in which to promptly localise and attack a submarine.

The most potent ASW weapons are SSNs, or nuclear-powered 'hunter-killer' submarines. In the Soviet navy, SSNs are used primarily to protect their SSBN fleet and major surface ships. NATO SSNs, on the other hand, operate independently and would be used for both anti-SSN and anti-SSBN operations, and to a lesser extent against surface ships. In 1981 the US navy had 43 SSNs in its Atlantic Fleet (half of its total force). Under an unprecedented SSN building programme the US navy aims to achieve a total fleet of 100 by 1990. These will be armed from 1984 not only with torpedoes, anti-submarine and anti-ship missiles but also nuclear and conventional cruise missiles for attacking land targets. These vessels may use Holy Loch's repair facilities, while the US navy communications station at Forss/West Murkle is already a vital element in command and control of SSN operations. Britain and France are also engaged in an unprecedented expansion of their SSN fleets.

Western SSNs are designed to operate in the 'high threat environment' of waters of US strategic interest close to the USSR, notably the Barents Sea. Both the US and British navies are believed to be very active in this region. In arms control terms the US SSN force is another 'destabilising' element since the current build-up and growing emphasis on 'forward area' operations by these vessels is likely to undermine Soviet faith in their nuclear retaliation capacity. This is well known to the US government and has been conceded in official statements.[20]

Taken as a whole – surveillance and detection systems, data processing and relay capabilities, weapons platforms and the weapons themselves – ASW is a major part of the USA's increasing orientation towards first strike capability. Many of these systems are, however, dependent on airfields, ports, fuel and weapons dumps, C^3I and navigation facilities, which are so numerous in Scotland and Scandinavia. This dependence suggests that a withdrawal of US basing rights by these countries, which have little or no say in superpower arms control talks, might go some way to arresting the destabilisation of the North Atlantic.

The US Ocean Surveillance Master Plan

In order to receive, process, evaluate and disseminate the vast inflow of surveillance and intelligence data received from all the sources described above, and that provided by bases like Edzell, and link it to weapons systems, the USA has established a global c^3 system which is intended to assist decision-making by the White House, the Pentagon and naval unit commanders. This is not merely limited to ASW but is essential to 'counter-force'. This system has at its hub the ASW Command and Control Centres System (ASWCCCS) and the Ocean Surveillance Information System (OSIS). ASWCCCS provides the secure data-processing, integration of all ASW systems and interconnection between lower level facilities (such as those on aircraft carriers) and higher command authorities (such as the Chief of Naval Operations). The OSIS integrates all the data sources and has links into the ASWCCCS and to national commands. It provides US Fleet Commanders-in-Chief with processed all-source intelligence and surveillance data on a worldwide basis. It can reveal at the push of a few buttons, for example, the disposition of all Soviet SSBNS and relevant details of each.

To handle its 'expanding battle space' the US navy is spending $1,500 million over the next few years in developing the Integrated Tactical Surveillance System (ITSS), which further combines all US airborne, satellite, ship and undersea sensors. Other sub-systems such as the Tactical Flag Command Centre (TFCC) provide commanders at sea with data from OSIS in addition to that from their own vessel's sensors.

Reinforcing a European war: Scotland's role

Until the late 1960s NATO's 'mutually assured destruction' strategy assumed that any war would be short and total. Since then the adoption of 'flexible response', and the steady development of weapons and force structures suited to such a strategy, have produced a growing stress on war-fighting capabilities. A vital element of this is America's ability to send massive reinforcements across the Atlantic in time of war. Following their experience of logistic support for wars in Vietnam and the Middle East, US military mobility is now well developed. Under Reagan, it is planned to make US forces capable of global intervention:

> Our long-term goal is to be able to meet the demands of a worldwide war, including concurrent reinforcement of Europe, deployments to South-west Asia (SWA) and the Pacific, and support for other areas.[21]

Britain would be vital for US reinforcement operations to Europe, acting both as a rearward base out of range of most Soviet combat aircraft and as the first European landfall for aircraft and ships crossing the Atlantic. The scale of this planned reinforcement is immense:

> Our ports and airfields provide important operational bases and would be key assembly, transit and launching points for the reinforcement of NATO's forces on the Continent, which would include moving well over a million men and their equipment from North America.[22]

To conduct this enormous operation, the USA is boosting its strategic cargo airlift capacity by 53 per cent by 1989, while the stockpiles of equipment pre-positioned in West Germany, Belgium and Holland for use by incoming US army reinforcements are being doubled in order to free cargo ships and aircraft for carrying additional supplies.

The vast US air armada will require the use of every available airfield in Europe. Prestwick would relive its Second World War role as one of the main termini for US military aircraft crossing the Atlantic. Any airfield in Scotland with a runway of 5,000 feet or more would also be earmarked. These would be used as trans-shipment points, with C-5s, C-141s and requisitioned civil aircraft landing from the USA and transferring their cargo to C-130s and other medium-range transports for onward journeys to the Continent.

Also crossing the Atlantic would be a constant stream of US combat aircraft reinforcements. By 1988 the Pentagon aims to be able to move 60 tactical fighter squadrons (the term 'tactical fighter' includes theatre nuclear bombers such as the F-111 and F-16) to Europe within 10 days, increasing the number of USAF aircraft here from about 750 in peacetime to 2,500 or more. Stockpiles of equipment for these squadrons are being established at 73 'co-located operating bases' (NATO airfields earmarked for USAF use) in Europe to save transporting it from the USA in wartime.

Air traffic control of these air reinforcements would be carried out from the Oceanic Control Centre at Prestwick, using data from NATS and RAF radar stations all over Scotland, particularly those at Sandwick, Benbecula and Tiree.

Under NATO plans, a prolonged war in Europe could not be sustained merely with reinforcement by air. Some 90–95 per cent of war supplies would go by sea, the first cargoes reaching Europe about 10 days after mobilisation. With considerable experience of seaborne supply of wars in Vietnam, the Middle East and the Falklands, Britain and the USA now have highly developed arrangements for the requisitioning of merchant ships and ports for military use. The Pentagon subsidises ship-owners to build military cargo capability into their most efficient vessels, the price for this being immediate requisitioning when required under the Maritime Appropriations Authorisation Act. Under US pressure, European members of NATO have also earmarked 600 of their merchant ships for military use. In Britain the military role of the Merchant Navy was well established long before Port Stanley became a household name. Sir Ronald Swayne, chairman of Overseas Containers Ltd, remarked in 1981 that 'we ship-owners work extremely closely with government (and always have done) in planning for defence.'[23]

The two main Scottish ports earmarked for military use are Greenock and Grangemouth. In addition, NATO emergency anchorages around the Scottish coast would be used, and many other locations will have been identified by the Admiralty and

Merchant Navy for unloading military cargo arriving from the USA. Sir Ronald Swayne has said:

> We are working on the difficult problems of emergency port anchorages, and . . . on the provision of lighters and preparation of places ashore which will take the heavy loads of a 40-ton container.[24]

Just as air traffic control is vital to air reinforcement, so naval control of shipping would be established to control convoy movements in UK waters. This role is carried out by the Royal Naval Reserve. Their port HQ at Lerwick would control supply ships moving from the Atlantic into the North Sea.

Civil air transport in NATO countries is also heavily militarised, just as Aeroflot serves the Soviet military. By 1982, 90 per cent of the USA's long-range civil airliners and every one of its long-range civil cargo planes were earmarked for military use as part of the Civil Reserve Air Fleet. Similar arrangements exist in Britain, and in 1981 Defence Secretary John Nott instructed his civil servants to devise a scheme for ensuring that new British civil airliners had built-in military cargo capability.[25]

Scotland also has a major role to play in reinforcing NATO's Northern Flank. While the USA is pursuing a new offensive policy in this region, designed to threaten Soviet forces in the Kola Peninsula, Norway's and Denmark's policies of refusing to have permanent foreign military bases in peacetime limit NATO's ability to match their forward naval deployments in the area with ground and air forces. To overcome this, in 1980 the Norwegians were forced to accept stockpiles of equipment for up to 20,000 British, Dutch and American marines, and over 200 US Marine Corps aircraft which would reinforce Norway in wartime. At the same time NATO has been seeking a permanent base for Norway-assigned US marines in the UK. There are numerous references to this, including a suggestion that the new base, and a new 'Arctic Command' headquarters, could be located in Shetland.[26] This would enable reinforcement of Norway in a matter of days rather than weeks.

Even without such a base, Scotland would still play a major part in supporting the deployment of US marines to Norway and

Denmark. One senior RAF officer sought to justify the £40 million airbase expansion at Stornoway by saying that US Marine Corps Air Wings (over 100 aircraft each)

> will require staging facilities in the UK before proceeding forward . . . Stornoway's enhanced facilities would afford us much needed additional staging facilities.[27]

Airfields in Shetland would also be used by British Harriers and helicopters en route to Norway with the UK Mobile Force.

It has been claimed that transatlantic reinforcement would become more important if NATO's reliance on nuclear weapons in Europe was reduced, since more conventional forces would be required. However, there are no signs that NATO is seeking to move away from its reliance on nuclear weapons, despite the much-publicised claims to the contrary by General Bernard Rogers, NATO's Supreme Allied Commander Europe (SACEUR).[28] Reinforcement in fact has little to do with substituting conventional weapons for nuclear. It is an integral part of the US drive for global mobility for their forces, making them capable of rapid intervention anywhere in the world and, by establishing stockpiles of equipment and weapons in 'host' countries such as Scotland and Norway, able to sustain operations in a protracted war.

Command, control, communications and intelligence

The extent to which the USA, NATO and the USSR could control and manage any war, but particularly a nuclear war, is dependent on the effectiveness and 'survivability' of the command, control, communications and intelligence (c^3i) links between commanders, forces and sensors. Most communications systems are highly vulnerable in wartime. Aerials and antennae can be destroyed by blast, electronic equipment can be damaged by the electro-magnetic pulse (EMP) from a nuclear explosion, and radio systems can be jammed by enemy electronic counter-measures (ECM). Disruption to power supplies is a further threat to c^3i systems.

The military has attempted to overcome these problems by

'hardening' communications equipment against blast, EMP and ECM, but above all by building 'redundancy' into their c^3I networks. This means that in the event of one or several links being destroyed or jammed, others can be switched in to maintain the link. The result is that the military (and associated civil) communications networks have many times the capacity actually required. This is well illustrated in Scotland, which has a plethora of bases associated with c^3I and a number of communications systems, both 'tactical' and 'strategic', ranging right across the radio frequency spectrum (see chapter 4).

Perhaps the most important of the c^3I systems in Scotland is UKADGE – the UK Air Defence Ground Environment. This is the system of radar sites, command and control centres and communications systems which provide air surveillance of the UK Air Defence Region (UKADR). The latter extends northwards to beyond the Faeroes and is part of the larger NATO Early Warning Area 12. Since 1972 UKADGE has been undergoing a major update and re-equipment. Airborne early warning Shackleton aircraft were based at Lossiemouth to improve detection of low-flying aircraft and to increase radar cover. A new RAF radar station was established at Benbecula. Coverage was further extended by integrating 'civil' NATS radars with UKADGE, and a new communications system is being introduced which makes Sector Operations Centres (SOCS), such as RAF Buchan, more capable of independent operation. Command bunkers such as the central one at High Wycombe are also being improved or replaced to make them less vulnerable to attack. The new Nimrod AEW.3 and US/NATO E-3 AWACS (Airborne Warning and Control System) aircraft will also be linked to UKADGE by an unjammable data link, enabling any elements in the system to communicate directly with each other.

UKADGE is fully interconnected with NADGE (NATO Air Defence Ground Environment). There is evidence that through these links, data from the UK air defence network are passed back to the USA via the North Atlantic Relay System (NARS), which passes through Mormond Hill. US commanders could use this information to monitor and direct overall military air operations in Europe.[29]

NADGE consists of 84 radar installations stretching from north Norway to Turkey, linked by communications systems such as ACE HIGH. Several upgrading projects are under way. The NATO Air Command and Control System (NACCS) will be operational in 1984. It is a NATO-wide system for command and control of offensive and defensive aircraft. It will link control centres ashore and afloat with surveillance sensors and weapons systems.[30] Under the NAEGIS (NATO Airborne Early Warning Ground Environment Integration Segment) programme, equipment is being installed at 41 NADGE radar sites, including Saxa Vord, to enable the NATO AEW force to exchange data with ground stations, ships and other aircraft.[31]

The NATO AEW force (11 RAF Nimrod AEW.3s and 18 NATO E-3A AWACS) is officially a defensive system, for improving the detection of attacking aircraft at long range and low altitude. However, one RAF officer has noted that 'an important feature of the concept is that it is not limited solely to defence',[32] while another stated that AEW 'complements defence suppression assets.'[33] AEW aircraft can be used to detect enemy electronic emissions and direct attack forces to these targets. They can also be used for communications jamming, as in 1982 when Israeli E-2Cs were used against the Syrian air force over Lebanon.

The AWACS is a vital component of General Rogers' plan for deep strikes on Warsaw Pact territory, and the maritime version, the E-3C, will be used by the USAF to pass target information to B-52s for anti-shipping strikes – a further element in NATO superiority in the North Atlantic.[34] Similarly, AEW Shackletons from Lossiemouth are already used to direct Buccaneers to their shipping targets.

Wilkes and Gleditsch suggest four main reasons why NADGE cannot exist for its official purpose of wartime air defence. Firstly, it is obsolete since it cannot detect low-flying aircraft; secondly it is unnecessary since ballistic missile attack is more likely than bomber attack; thirdly, it cannot detect missiles; and finally it is highly vulnerable due to the need to protect both radar and communications aerials.[35]

For these reasons NADGE would be of most use as a peacetime surveillance instrument, monitoring Warsaw Pact training flights and operational mission patterns as an aid to NATO war planning. In wartime, NADGE could be used to monitor NATO attacks or counter-attacks on the USSR.

Wilkes and Gleditsch's conclusions apply equally to UKADGE. Despite the increasing orientation of UKADGE to the north and west, there is little evidence that the USSR is able or willing to mount manned aircraft attacks against the UK, particularly from these directions. UKADGE, particularly in Scotland, would be of most use in ensuring the safe transit of air reinforcements from the USA. For this purpose 'it is able to cope with the massive influx of US combat aircraft into the UK in times of tension or war.'[36] UKADGE, supposedly the UK's national air defence system, cannot be separated from the UK's wartime role as a rearward base for military forces fighting a war in Europe. Some form of national air defence system is desirable, but a purely defensive system would look very different from UKADGE or NADGE.

2. Military expansion in perspective

In some respects, the military is less prominent in Scotland than it used to be. Since the abolition of national service in 1962 the British armed services have relied on a relatively small professional, all-volunteer force, but one which, because of more intensive training and high technology equipment, is far more efficient at killing people (more 'firepower-intensive'). At the same time, as the emphasis has moved from manpower to equipment, the demand for large tracts of land for infantry and other field training has contracted overall. This is reflected in the statistics of defence land holdings. During the Second World War, the military held about 11.5 million acres of land in Britain (about 20 per cent of the UK land area); by 1947 this was down to about a million acres, and following the reappraisal of defence land holdings in 1972–73 by the Nugent Committee, declined to its present total of around 700,000 acres.[1]

Within these trends, however, there have been a number of important changes of direction in British and NATO military policy which can be seen in the post-war history of the Scottish military presence. After a brief but rapid contraction immediately after the Second World War, the massive rearmament in the Korean war period led to reactivation of many military installations in Scotland, particularly airfields and naval facilities, in the early 1950s. By that time the Pentagon was building up US military facilities in Britain, while Britain's continued emphasis on a strong navy for intervention across the globe was reflected in the expansion or retention of virtually all the wartime naval facilities in Scotland. The most important change in British policy, however, was the 1957 Defence White Paper, which reflected Britain's achievement of full 'independent' nuclear capability, and the predominant strategic thinking of the time that the USSR was to be contained by the threat of massive nuclear retaliation. The 1957 White Paper abolished conscription and reduced conventional forces overall; RAF Fighter Command was reduced in size as manned aircraft were seen to be obsolete in the missile age, and much of the radar network was to be abandoned as it was ill-suited to defence against nuclear attack. The traditional power of the navy lobby meant that it survived the 1957 cuts in conventional forces by 'discovering' a new role as imperial policeman East of Suez, but in the Atlantic the move to a short nuclear war strategy meant a reduction in surface ships and growing emphasis on submarines and hence anti-submarine warfare.

However, the 'poodle' syndrome was already well-established as the 1957 defence policy changes were taking effect. US policy, which had always included a substantial war-fighting element, and in 1962 officially adopted such a stance, was at odds with Britain's attempts to reduce conventional forces and maintain an 'independent' nuclear capability. This could not, and did not, last for long – the rest of NATO was dragged into America's policy of establishing both the ability and the will to fight a 'limited' nuclear war in Europe. It is important to recognise the effect this had on the military presence in Scotland. The largest peacetime military expansion in Scotland occurred in the period 1958–63: the airfields at Prestwick, Lossiemouth, Stornoway and Machrihanish were redeveloped; Holy Loch handed to the US navy; naval fuel depots built at Campbeltown, Rosneath, Loch Striven and Aultbea; the boom defence depot at Fairlie established; and a string of American command, control, communications and intelligence (C^3I) installations constructed – Forss/West Murkle, Mormond Hill and the related ACE HIGH stations in Shetland, Edzell and the US navy's UK Microwave System. Most of these new bases were funded entirely by NATO, and despite the trends in British policy towards a 'massive nuclear retaliation' strategy, most of them were unquestionably directed towards the ability to conduct a protracted war. This is not true of the original ACE HIGH C^3I system but is certainly the case with the naval fuel or

POL (petroleum, oil and lubricants) depots, which provided the two main navies in the Atlantic, the Royal Navy and US navy, with the means to operate for long periods at sea by refuelling from military tankers which could take on fuel at Invergordon, Scapa Flow and the new west-coast depots for transfer to warships at sea. This coincided with the introduction of the US navy's first two 80,000 ton-class aircraft carriers, USS *Kittyhawk* and USS *Constellation*, in 1961; these formed the spearhead of the NATO Strike Fleet Atlantic (STRKFLTLANT) which would be used to attack Soviet strategic bases at Kola. The new fuel depots also fitted in with a long war strategy in Europe by supporting the escort ships needed to protect transatlantic reinforcement convoys.

Support for US navy aircraft carriers in the Atlantic was also the original rationale for the expansion at Stornoway and Machrihanish in this period. Throughout 1958 and 1959, Supreme Allied Commander Atlantic (SACLANT) plans envisaged both bases being used to accommodate, refuel, rearm and maintain the 80–90 aircraft of each carrier. Major NATO maritime exercises in this period (such as 'Strikeback' in 1957) involved as many as five aircraft carriers in Scottish waters, and since one airfield could only accommodate one carrier's aircraft, several locations would be required. However, in 1960 it was announced that, although the developments at both Stornoway and Machrihanish were to go ahead, they were to function not as shore bases for STRKFLTLANT's aircraft but as reserve or forward operating bases for long-range maritime patrol and anti-submarine aircraft. It is believed that this was a result of the US and Norwegian governments reaching agreement in 1960 on a programme dubbed 'INVICTUS' which gave the US navy rights to develop certain Norwegian airfields as wartime forward operating bases or shore support facilities for the combat aircraft from its carriers. US success in persuading Norway that 'INVICTUS' was not in contravention of their policy of no foreign military bases reduced the requirement for similar bases in Scotland, one thousand miles further away from the intended battlefield.

This illustrates another worrying aspect of military expansionism in Scotland and elsewhere – the ability of a highly structured and internationally organised military bloc like NATO to play off one country against another in its war preparations. Similar methods have been used recently; after discussions between the British and American governments in 1978 aimed at obtaining a forward base in Britain for Norway-assigned US marines,[2] the Norwegians agreed in late 1980 to accept the stockpiling of equipment in central Norway for an entire USMC brigade and its air wing. The next step is likely to be a US argument that this is not enough, and that for the marines to use this stockpile effectively they must be permanently based closer to it than the east coast of the USA – almost certainly in Scotland. Again, with the proposed expansion at Stornoway, NATO strategists evidently felt it necessary to guard against any resurgence of nationalist or anti-militarist sentiments in Iceland by ensuring that at least some of the US forces there would have an alternative base in Scotland. The chances of NATO success in countering opposition in one North Atlantic country by expanding in another remain high as long as peace campaigns focus on single issues and lack the means to link these related campaigns in other countries. Scotland, with its plethora of military installations related to anti-submarine warfare (ASW) and other military activity in the North Atlantic, has a major role to play in developing this opposition on an international basis.

The expansion of the Scottish military presence in the late 1950s and early 1960s was not, however, entirely related to the North Atlantic. The setting up of the army ranges at South Uist and Kirkcudbright, for firing tactical nuclear missiles and tank guns respectively, were related primarily to the changes in NATO strategy in Central Europe; once again, despite the official British stance of planning for a short, all-out war, these bases directly represented the already well-established American moves towards the ability to fight a 'limited' nuclear war.

Also in this period, the UK Warning and Monitoring Organisation (UKWMO) was giving some credibility to the nuclear fall-out warning role of the Royal Observer Corps (ROC) by establishing a network of monitoring posts and bunkers for their group and sector controls throughout Britain. The construction of four monitoring posts in Lewis and Harris in 1962 completed the UK network, and six group control bunkers for the ROC in Scotland, plus the Caledonian sector bunker at Dundee, were also built in 1961–62, three of them in renovated RAF fighter control bunkers. For the first five years of the existence of this network, its prime function was to warn the public of nuclear attack, but following the official NATO adoption of 'flexible response', the disbanding of the Civil Defence Corps and the abandonment in 1967–68 of plans to evacuate the civil population in the event of war, the ROC went through a five-year period of reorganisation which switched its emphasis from pre-attack warning to the public to a survivable nuclear burst, fall-out and upper atmosphere forecasting system designed to advise the military on dispersal of their forces – in short, a war-fighting role. Emphasis was placed on telecommunications, and in Scotland the ROC's 27 Group at Connel was disbanded, responsibility for its monitoring posts split between 30 Group (Inverness) and 25 Group (Prestwick), and the Connel bunker turned into a joint-services communications monitoring facility.[3]

With all this expansion going on, it is hardly surprising that rumours and speculation about military developments in Scotland were rife. In the Western Isles alone, the local press carried reports of the area being used for a Ballistic Missile Early Warning System (BMEWS) station, port facilities for West German naval patrol boats, low-flying training by the Luftwaffe, and a base for Polaris submarines. These were not entirely unfounded fears – the BMEWS communications station was subsequently built in Shetland, after testing some of its equipment at Stornoway in 1959–60, and the rumour of Luftwaffe low-flying in the area was based on an offer by the UK government to the Germans to provide these facilities (the offer was turned down on the grounds of the Western Isles' distance from West Germany and the unpredictability of the Hebridean weather).[4] Elsewhere in Scotland the news that the RAF was to acquire 60 Thor medium-range nuclear missiles (under dual control) in 1957–58 for basing in the UK led to speculation that they were to be based in north and east Scotland.[5] The disused military airfields at East Fortune (which had been under USAF control until 1955), Easthaven, Peterhead, Crimond and Banff would have been ideal sites. The missiles were, however, based in eastern England.

There is some evidence to suggest that rumours of major expansion by the military are initiated deliberately by the MOD in order to prepare the public for official announcements of new developments. In several cases, while initial rumours have suggested large-scale military bases, the eventual development has actually been on a much smaller scale – the public's reaction being relief at the apparent reduction in the military's plans. The most recent example of this was the scaling-down of the expansion plans for Coulport for the Trident missile. A more telling illustration of the process, however, is the recent history of the NATO developments at Stornoway. Having obtained a 'foot in the door' in the early 1960s by establishing minimum facilities at Stornoway airport for the operation of maritime patrol aircraft, and after their largely unnoticed purchase of the land in and around the airfield in 1973, the MOD were in a good position from which to expand without drawing too much attention to themselves. However, their initial £6 million proposals in 1977 rapidly escalated to £20 million by early 1980, and within a few months to £40 million.[6] This gave rise to fears that it was to become a major new base, and certainly fuelled the already well-organised opposition. Yet by the time of the public inquiry in March 1981, the MOD had scaled down their plans considerably – since 1979 the amount of new paving to be laid on the airfield was reduced by two-thirds (including the deletion of two emergency runways); the number of married quarters reduced from 20 to 8; barrack accommodation reduced from a maximum of 100 men to 22; hardened aircraft shelters reduced from 12 to 9; and the fuel jetty and undersea pipeline in Loch a'Tuath deleted from the plans. The only thing which did not change was the cost – £40 million. Since one of the main reasons for any local support for the military expansion at Stornoway was job creation, it was plainly in the MOD's interests to publicise an overestimate of the likely construction work. The MOD had already attracted the interest of the large number of unemployed construction workers in the islands by referring to a peak labour force of 450, but the figures quoted by the Property Services Agency's Development Manager for the Stornoway project at the public inquiry demonstrated that the recruitment of local labour would be only of the order of 50–100 jobs, all of them seasonal.[7]

It would be wrong to claim that these alterations in the Stornoway plans were purely designed to pacify local opposition by reducing the scale of the original proposals; undoubtedly one of the major factors involved was the MOD's concern to get as much of their plans financed by the NATO Infrastructure Programme as possible, in which case it would make sense to ask for more than was needed in the hope of the essential elements being approved. Furthermore, the financial difficulties of the NATO Infrastructure Programme since 1980 and the inflation caused by a five-year delay in the construction programme undoubtedly forced the MOD to scale down their plans. Nevertheless there remains a cynical side to the history of the Stornoway expansion. The MOD admitted in 1979 that among the major functions of an expanded Stornoway airbase would be use by NATO maritime patrol aircraft and support for US air reinforcement of Europe; yet no NATO representatives were present at the inquiry, and RAF witnesses stated consistently that the base was solely for RAF air defence operations and they 'simply didn't know' about use by other NATO air forces – clearly an attempt to dispel local fears of a foreign military invasion.

Rumour and speculation is an inevitable part of predicting military expansion, since plans are kept secret until they are ready for implementation, and the military have wide-ranging powers to buy up land or expand existing bases with virtually no accountability to the public. However, it is important to be able to differentiate between rumour and reality. The most common rumours of military expansion in Scotland concern new bases for Polaris, Poseidon or Trident submarines. Rumours abound of new bases for this purpose being considered at Stornoway, Lochmaddy, Kishorn and Portavadie, and while it is true that the US navy's SSBN facilities at Holy Loch are highly mobile – the mother ship could be moved to virtually any sea loch on the west coast without much difficulty – the scale of the support organisation needed for a nuclear missile submarine base such as Faslane/Coulport is so great that there is no prospect of it being moved, particularly to an island site where road and rail communications are difficult or impossible. On the other hand, expansion at existing bases often passes unopposed because local people accept at face value the reassurances of local base commanders and MOD spokespeople. Hence at Holy Loch in late 1982 the district council were taken in by the assurances of Commander Fred Krafft, US navy, that expansion of shore facilities in Sandbank was 'consolidation, not expansion',[8] apparently unaware of the background of the largest ever peacetime expansion of the US navy and the deployment of over 3,000 cruise missiles on board US ships and submarines, many of them operating in the North Atlantic. Down the Clyde at Machrihanish an £11 million expansion of base facilities is under way, and again MOD statements claiming that this is not an upgrading of the base seem to have been largely accepted. The lesson is clear – unhindered military expansionism can only be challenged effectively if both the peace movement and the local authorities responsible for approving military developments in their area are fully aware of the strategic background to these developments and the precise function of each military base.

The 'Keep NATO Out' campaign in Stornoway, which resulted from a local teacher happening to notice a tiny piece of paper announcing the MOD's intentions pinned to a fence on the edge of the airfield, has demonstrated the importance of monitoring all MOD planning applications to local authorities. Since this is frequently the only element of public accountability in military expansion plans it can be a vital step in the opposition to militarisation. The success of the campaign for local authorities to declare themselves nuclear-free gives added hope, as do efforts of Comhairle nan Eilean (the Western Isles Council) and Strathclyde Regional Council to break the bounds of local planning inquiries by arguing for discussion and debate of the wider strategic aspects of military development proposals.

Unfortunately the planning system cannot cope with much of the current military expansion going on in Scotland, since it is largely qualitative not quantitative. In particular, civil authorities have no say over the introduction of new weapons at military bases or the development of war-fighting capabilities such as the 'hardening' programmes at Leuchars and Lossiemouth.

Over the next few years these qualitative developments will be at the core of any military expansion in Scotland. NATO satellite communications links and new MOD communications systems such as BOXER, UNITER and MOULD are already being extended into Scotland, while automated data processing and message switching systems at the various command, control, communications and intelligence bases in Scotland will boost their capacity several-fold.

The other major facet of military expansion in Scotland is the current government's emphasis on 'home defence'. The Falklands war demonstrated the use of the army's 5th Infantry Brigade in its rapid overseas deployment role, but little has been said about its primary role, which is home defence. Additional TAVR units and the new Home Service Force (HSF) are being formed to guard 'key points' such as telephone exchanges and power stations in wartime, officially against the Soviet equivalent of the SAS. However, 'the main threat is dissident Britons'.[9] Quite apart from their wartime role, these new reservist units will consolidate pro-military attitudes in a substantial section of the civil population.

3. The armed society: the impact of the military in Scotland

Since 1979 British military spending has been rising by 4.3 per cent a year. In the same period we have been experiencing a disastrous recession. The arms manufacturers are among the few industries which show increasing turnover and profits. In Scotland, where the effects of economic crisis bite particularly deeply, many areas are becoming more reliant on military industries and bases for their economic survival. Many people welcome the employment and income created in this way, irrespective of its source. But although many individuals benefit from the presence of a military base in their locality, the overall social and economic benefits of the military presence are highly questionable.

Major military bases, particularly in Scotland, tend to be located in rural areas, well away from the large towns and cities. This can lead to a dependence on the military as a source of local employment. For example, the 1,950 service personnel and 280 civilian workers at RAF Kinloss in 1979 made up no less than 41 per cent of the total labour force in the Forres area.[1] However, an earlier study found that the civilian employment at the two Moray airbases amounted to only 4 per cent of employment in the county.[2]

Not much of this employment is locally recruited, and what is does not fill the more skilled jobs. Military establishments, particularly airfields and operational naval bases such as Faslane, involve increasingly sophisticated technology, and many of the required skills are not available locally. Furthermore, for security reasons and because of the military's own self-interest in being self-sufficient in skilled labour, most civilian defence jobs are unskilled or semi-skilled, and relatively low paid – 'not quite wholly servants, cooks and bottle-washers, but very largely that'.[3]

The present government is accelerating the already significant shedding of civilian jobs in defence. MOD civilian employment has declined from 391,400 in 1967 to around 210,000 in 1983, with a target of less than 190,000 by 1987.[4] At Faslane, security worries following strikes by civilian employees responsible for Polaris missiles in 1977, 1978 and 1981 led to the loss of up to 400 jobs at the base from 1982. Many of these posts are now filled by service personnel.[5] The drive towards privatisation in the civil service is also having a severe impact on MOD civilian employment. In 1982–83, 16 per cent of the civil workforce at the South Uist missile range lost their jobs when cleaning work was taken over by a private contractor.

All these elements combine to make civilian defence jobs far less secure than in the past, and in most cases the jobs that *are* provided are restricted to menial tasks which offer little in the way of advancement.

Effects on the local economy

Military bases contribute little to the local economy. Their centrally organised supply system buys very little locally, and since the military does not produce anything there are no spin-offs to local industry. Even massive increases in the value of capital equipment have little spillover into the local economy. The introduction of the Nimrod MR.2 at Kinloss from 1979 added over £150 million to the value of equipment on the airfield but contibuted nothing to the economy of the area.

Most studies of the economic impact of military bases suggest that for every 100 jobs (service personnel and directly-employed civilians) created at a base there are between 20 and 60 jobs indirectly generated in the local economy. Studies done in the USA and in Scotland have shown that a private export industry generates twice as many jobs elsewhere in the local economy as an airbase.[6] Military establishments may actually reduce the prospects for industrial or other economic developments locally since they absorb much of the labour and other resources which might otherwise encourage economic development.

The same economists' studies show that the multiplier effect for income is even lower than that for employment – between 1.2 and 1.35 for Kinloss and Lossiemouth, or £20,000–£35,000 additional income for every £100,000 paid out to service personnel and civil employees. Most military bases provide for a large proportion of the needs of their personnel on the base itself – housing, clothing, food and drink, recreation, transport and in the case of many us bases, education too. At Holy Loch,

> local tradesmen have hardly benefited from the 'invading forces', who do their food shopping in the Commissary, a non-profit making supermarket run by the us government, where prime beef costs about half the local going rate.[7]

Despite the fact that military bases pay a contribution to rates, the local area often ends up effectively subsidising the bases. Local authorities find themselves forced into expensive projects, while in some areas many local services are overstretched by the demands of the military.

In South Uist, senior officers at the missile range are always keen to point out the base's economic contributions – a £210,000 contribution to the new £1.6 million causeway from Benbecula to South Uist, a 40 per cent share in the cost of a new power station at Carnan, financial aid for the building of the new Balivanich primary school, 10 per cent of their rates contribution earmarked for road maintenance, and a £2 million strengthening of the runway at Benbecula airfield in 1977. These should be put in perspective. Much of the road traffic in the Uists, particularly across South Ford causeway, is military, so a 13 per cent share in the causeway's cost is a bargain. The army is a major consumer of power in the islands, and in 1972 it built a costly 1 mile long power line to a radar station in North Uist when the township of Lochportain still had no mains electricity. About 70 per cent of the children at Balivanich school are from army families. Most dishonest, however, is the claim that the runway strengthening is a service to the community. This work was only required because the army transports missiles and personnel to Benbecula in RAF Hercules transports which are more than three times the weight of the British Airways HS.748s which operate the civil air service from Glasgow. Even these HS.748s are an extravagance. The only reason for operating this size of aircraft on the Benbecula route is that the army accounts for 60 per cent of the traffic on the route. The need to maintain unnecessarily long and strengthened runways due to the military presence is one of the reasons for Benbecula airport's huge losses at public expense.

Undeniably, military bases frequently provide services not otherwise available to the local community. However, local dependence on electricity, water supplies or roads built for the military is a handy tool for manipulating local opinion when expansion is planned. In any case, the rates paid to local authorities by military establishments are relatively insignificant when viewed on a regional scale. In Highland Region the biggest military rates payments come from the naval fuel depots at Aultbea and Invergordon. They each paid between £150,000 and £200,000 in 1981–82. However, Invergordon may close in 1986, and the 'benefit' to the people of Aultbea includes having to accept an MOD ban on planning developments in the area. Bases like Tain Range, which have few buildings, pay very little in rates despite their enormous environmental impact.

Overall, the military only contributes about 1.5 per cent of Highland Region's rates income. When one considers the military's swallowing up of land, airspace, fishing grounds, potentially productive labour, housing and other resources, and the disturbance caused by low-flying aircraft and all manner of explosions in the region, this is meagre compensation.

The land issue

Although the military's land holdings in Scotland are small in relation to total land area (the MOD owns, leases and has rights over some 75,000 acres of land in Scotland[8]) the impact of defence land use at a local level is great. Moreover, military training and exercises take place on land, sea and in the air over virtually the entire country.

The most notable feature of military land use in Scotland is the number of bases which are unique, and justified for their uniqueness, particularly in terms of Scotland's geographical attributes. Cape Wrath is 'the only ship-to-shore bombardment range in Europe';[9] Holy Loch is currently the only foreign SSBN base in the world, while BUTEC and the Uist missile range have been described as the only facilities of their kind in Europe.

Current plans to develop or expand the bases at Holy Loch, South Uist and the Sound of Raasay are all taking place against a background of strings of promises of no further expansion. Technological developments mean that increasing land requirements for existing bases are less likely in future, but in many areas even a few acres of land swallowed up for military use may drastically alter the viability of crofts and farms or a local community's prospects for industrial development.[10]

The land issue does not relate solely to areas which the MOD owns, leases or has rights over. Full-scale field exercises cannot be accommodated on most MOD training areas. To overcome this, privately-owned estates are used by all kinds of military units, from army cadets to US Naval Special Warfare troops. The military depends on the goodwill of estate-owners for the use of their land for exercises, and here the regimental tie comes into its own. Allen Garry's study revealed that 32.6 per cent of Highland land-owners were retired military officers who retain their military rank.[11] In many cases their retention of military rank also signifies retention of links with the military through regimental associations, personal friends, business contacts and service in the Territorials or Reserves. Through these largely informal links with the military, land-owners provide free training facilities for the MOD across vast acreages, with no reference to the wishes of local people.

Public consultation is rare even when these exercises involve blatant infringement of civil liberties. In October 1979, an exercise involving local police and London-based SAS reservists took place in Morayshire. Locals were stopped and interrogated at road blocks in the Elgin/Lossiemouth area. One MOD spokesman said afterwards, 'We received a lot of useful information, particularly from the road-block checks.'[12]

Commandos, SAS and other 'special' units have traditionally trained in Scotland. Colonel David Stirling, founder of the wartime SAS and the neo-fascist 'GB 75' private army and owner of Morar estate, and his neighbours Lord Lovat (of the Lovat Scouts) and Major W.G. Gordon (of gin fame) are particular enthusiasts of elite military units training on their land, which was also a major training ground for commandos and Special Operations Executive underground agents in the Second World War. The SAS makes regular use of the 'adventure training centre' at Ardentigh on Loch Nevis run by ex-SAS man 'Moby' Maclean in association with Stirling and Gordon. The adjacent Knoydart estate narrowly escaped coming under military control in early 1983 when strong public opposition led to the new Defence Secretary, Michael Heseltine, announcing the withdrawal of the MOD's interest. The purchase would have more than doubled MOD land holdings in Scotland.

'Jet noise – the sound of freedom': military low-flying

The most audible military presence in rural Scotland is that of low-flying aircraft. There are regular complaints about noise disturbing old people, children and livestock, and in some cases for it being indirectly responsible for people's deaths. However, the importance of low-flying lies not merely in the fear and fright it causes. It is essential to understand why low-flying takes place at all, particularly the way in which it contributes to NATO's war-fighting strategy, and hence why it is important for low-flying to be opposed.

Scotland has a number of attractions as a low-flying area. Firstly, there is no controlled airspace, where all pilots must operate under air traffic control, north of central Scotland. Secondly, the mountainous terrain is ideal for low-level training in a 'realistic' environment; and finally there are four live bombing ranges which can be used as practice targets on low-level training flights. These attractions have become particularly significant over the last 15 years as NATO strategy has shifted from a reliance on massive nuclear retaliation to one of 'flexible response and forward defence', in which NATO strike/

attack aircraft are tasked to penetrate Warsaw Pact defences at low level and high speed to destroy 'theatre' or 'tactical' targets such as airfields, ports, military–industrial installations, supply lines and concentrations of military equipment, using both conventional and nuclear weapons.

Since the 1960s military aircraft designers have concentrated on the ability to fly and attack from a low level in order to avoid radar detection. The RAF in particular is now geared almost exclusively to low-level operations, with Jaguars and Harriers for close support of ground troops and Buccaneers and Tornados for longer-range offensive missions. This emphasis has had a marked effect on the use of low-flying areas, not only by the RAF but also the US and other NATO air forces which are also devoting more effort to lower and faster flying.

Many people imagine that the aircraft seen low-flying over Scotland are contributing to the defence of Britain. This is true only under a very loose definition of the term 'defence'. The vast majority of Scottish low-flyers are offensive aircraft training for nuclear and conventional attacks on targets in East Germany and the USSR. The heaviest users of Scottish low-flying areas are the RAF Jaguars and Buccaneers from Lossiemouth and other bases in England and Germany, and USAF F-111s from Upper Heyford and Lakenheath. In 1983 RAF Tornados were rapidly becoming a major presence. Other users of low-flying areas are extremely diverse – from Jet Provost basic trainers up to Hercules transports and USAF B-52 bombers.

Until January 1979 military low-flying in the UK was restricted to a number of designated areas within which aircraft could fly as low as 250 feet at up to 450 knots (511 miles per hour). The largest of these was Low-Flying Area 15, covering the entire Scottish mainland north of Oban and Montrose. By the late 1970s the MOD was looking for a means of meeting ever expanding low-level training requirements while appearing to respond to the growing number of complaints about low-flying disturbance and the increasing fears of many civil pilots about mid-air collisions.

From 1 January 1979 the entire area of the UK, with the exception of zones around major civil airports, military danger areas, and an area around the holiday towns on the Kent–Sussex coast, became available for military low-flying. Of the eight areas over land in Scotland which remained prohibited to low-flying, six were existing weapons ranges. The Western Isles were included in the low-flying area for the first time, with only Orkney and Shetland 'not normally available'. This enormous expansion was sold to the public by the then Labour defence minister as a spreading of the burden of disturbance from low-flying. In fact it was designed purely to allow for a burgeoning of low-level training and to remove existing restrictions from pilots.

Little publicity has been given to the progressive reduction in operating heights in some parts of the low-flying areas. This has come about as a result of US combat experience in Vietnam which showed the need for more realism in peacetime training. The result was the setting up of the Red Flag series of war games in the Nevada desert. The RAF has been participating in these since 1977. In order to practise the sort of flying carried out in Red Flag exercises, the RAF was allocated two special areas in north-west Scotland and central Wales where they were permitted to fly as low as 100 feet and at speeds well in excess of 500 knots. There was no public consultation about this move. Nor was the public informed about the designation of a further ultra-low-flying area covering 900 square miles of Angus, Kincardine and Deeside early in 1982.[13] There have even been false public statements from senior RAF officers. Seven months after the first use of the 100 ft area in north-west Scotland the air officer commanding 38 Group RAF said, 'I have been asked to look at the possibility of recommending the authorisation of flying down to 100 feet – but I don't think we will ever do that because of the low-flying sensitivity.'[14]

The safety aspects of flying as low as 100 feet are particularly disturbing. Pilots training to fly the Buccaneer, one of the main users of these special 100 ft areas, are forbidden to fly at less than 500 feet since the MOD insists it would be 'too difficult and dangerous',[15] but Buccaneers are regularly being flown over Scotland and Wales at a fifth of that height.

Contempt for public consultation has also been shown in the

setting up of the Highlands Restricted Area, a new low-flying area covering almost the entire mainland north of the Great Glen. This was established in October 1981 as the first ever permanent facility for blind-flying at low level in Europe. Its function is to allow RAF Tornado and USAF F-111 crews to practise low-flying at night and in bad weather, using terrain-following radar. When it was set up the official line was that none of the aircraft would be flying at less than 360 feet. No one was told that by early 1983 these aircraft would be flying regularly at 200 feet. The establishment of the Highlands Restricted Area angered and worried many local individuals and organisations. The chairperson of Sutherland District Council was moved to comment:

> We have been selected for this low-flying at night because of our sparse population and remoteness, and yet these factors are never remembered when they consider the effect on us of increased petrol charges, VAT or freight charges.[16]

Official figures for the amount of low-flying conducted over the UK demonstrate an increase over the period 1978 to 1981 of up to 100 per cent in the number of low-level flights per year. The total figure in 1983, including RAF, USAF and other NATO air forces, is estimated to be at least 150,000 flights over the UK every year, and rising.[17] The MOD says that about 16 per cent of these take place over Scotland (though this figure is thought to have risen since the establishment of the Highlands Restricted Area). This means that an average of 90 low-level flights take place over Scotland each weekday. Variations due to weather and exercises push the figure to over 250 on some days, while geographical concentration means that some areas such as Newton Stewart and Fort William suffer far more disturbance than others.

The RAF is notoriously silent about precisely how low-flying is controlled. This is because the details are too embarrassing to be made public. Low-flying in Scotland is controlled by a unit within the Scottish Air Traffic Control Centre (Military) at Prestwick which listens out on a specified UHF radio frequency. Aircraft entering the low-flying area make a radio call to this unit, giving their position. However, the air traffic control radio network cannot provide low-level UHF or VHF coverage of the Highlands, where most low-flying takes place, so the radio call may not be heard. Similarly there is no radar coverage of aircraft in low-flying areas. Once in the low-flying area, the onus is entirely on the pilot and navigator to maintain the planned route, keep the aircraft within the prescribed height and speed limits and avoid prohibited areas, radio masts, birds and other aircraft. Pilots are given no information on the whereabouts of other aircraft at low-level.

This almost total freedom for pilots once in the low-flying area is wide open to abuse. In 1981 a USAF F-111 pilot was fined £900 and sent back to the USA after being found guilty of illegal low-flying over his aunt's house in Deeside. Most RAF pilots, asked if they ever fly below the prescribed 250 ft minimum, will reply with a wry smile. Occasionally an accident reveals the extent of these breaches of the regulations. The most embarrassing one for the RAF was in April 1983, when a member of their elite 'Red Arrows' aerobatic team, apparently attempting to fly *under* a set of 132,000 volt power lines near Fort Augustus, hit the lower cable, some 30 feet off the ground. One of the occupants ejected but the pilot managed to land the badly damaged plane at Inverness. There then followed a rushed cover-up by the MOD, who claimed that the aircraft had not hit the power lines, let alone been damaged.

It has been said that military pilots are highly trained professionals whose high standards of integrity prevent any irresponsibility in the air. Anyone with no doubts about this should read a book by Robert Prest, for several years a Phantom pilot at Leuchars. He describes the climax of a low-level flight over southern Scotland as follows:

He is in my sights and I am following his random weaves . . . I ignore the thatched shepherd's cottage that appears from nowhere in the barrenness . . . I ignore the parked car and the white faces of a family sitting round a picnic table in the middle of nowhere, staring upwards. My finger flexes round the trigger, willing that toy in my gunsight to come closer, for the wing-tips to fill the 25-mil circle in my glowing gunsight.[18]

It is not surprising that operations at low level by fast jet aircraft involve accidents. Out of a total of 33 military air crashes in Scotland between March 1978 and March 1983, at least 57 per cent occurred in the course of low-level flights. There are also regular near misses between aircraft at low levels, though these are kept secret. The area around Aberdeen is notorious for unannounced intrusions by military aircraft into civil airspace. The managing director of Bristow Helicopters has referred to 'the appalling low-flying behaviour of military aircraft',[19] while a union official monitoring air safety around Aberdeen said, 'We heard of one air traffic controller holding up his hands in horror and saying he couldn't cope with all the military activity.'[20]

Of even greater concern is the possibility of a crash involving an aircraft carrying nuclear weapons. Many nuclear-capable aircraft have crashed in Scotland, and there is evidence that in May 1964 a USAF Voodoo from Bentwaters in Suffolk which crashed in Argyll was carrying a nuclear weapon.

The official complaints procedure for low-flying disturbance is well known as a farce in the worst affected areas. Any complaints about disturbance caused by aircraft flying within the official limits are deemed invalid, and each complaint must be accompanied by a description of the type, colour, serial number, direction and exact time of flight of the aircraft concerned if it is to be sure of attention.

NATO's concentration on strike/attack capability is directly responsible for the proliferation of low-flying in Scotland. A non-offensive security policy would bring with it a much quieter and safer life for rural Scots.

The unwanted catch

Naval and amphibious exercises off Scotland are a regular source of annoyance to fishermen both for the disruption caused to fishing activity and the frequent lack of consultation or notification. Resentment came to a head in autumn 1982 when static gear fishermen in Caithness only learned of plans to mount a landing of up to 2,500 US marines at Sinclair's Bay 10 days before the event, and this only through the local paper. This left insufficient time to lift creels to avoid damage by ships and landing craft. Land-owners and the oil industry had been notified up to a year in advance. The secretary of the Highlands and Islands Fishermen's Association commented: 'The Ministry of Defence have once again resorted to their steamrolling of the fishing industry.'[21]

The number of incidents involving fishing boats and torpedoes or submarines in Scottish waters is alarming. Virtually the entire Firth of Clyde and the Sound of Jura are submarine exercise areas, an activity not exactly conducive to safe fishing. In March 1979 a Campbeltown-based fishing boat caught an unexpectedly large fish when a US navy Poseidon SSBN (ballistic missile submarine) from Holy Loch ran into its nets in the Sound of Jura. The fishing boat was towed backwards at speed for 10 minutes before the crew could cut their trawl gear. They were extremely lucky not to be dragged underwater. The submarine did not slow down, surface or stop. The US navy later stated that one of their submarines had been in the area at the time.

Three years later the diesel patrol submarine HMS *Porpoise*, one of 16 such vessels in the Royal Navy used primarily for clandestine surveillance and Special Boat Squadron (SBS) operations, dragged an Irish trawler backwards for two miles and sank it, miraculously without loss of life. Again the submarine neither stopped, surfaced nor slowed down, and the British government took two weeks to admit responsibility, having first denied that any of their submarines were in the area. Soon afterwards a French trawler sank without trace in the Irish Sea. This was widely thought to be another victim of a submarine collision.

The detritus of preparations for underwater warfare is a further hazard in Scottish waters, particularly in the sea lochs of the Clyde where torpedo trials and practice firings are carried out. In one day alone in March 1981 no fewer than four separate incidents occurred in the Clyde in which fishing boats picked up torpedoes in their nets – one off Arran, two off Troon, the fourth in Loch Fyne.

The planning system – democratic control?

One of the few means of civilian control over military land use is the planning system. However, any agent of the crown intending to develop land, buildings or any other property is under no legal requirement to seek permission from the local planning authority. The only semblance of democracy is based on Scottish Development Department Circular 49/77, which provides that government developers should seek the views of local authorities on their plans. The local authority then considers the plans as it would a statutory planning application, with the crucial difference that their views can be completely ignored by the government if it does not agree with them. In Scotland, the Secretary of State then has overall jurisdiction and can decide whether or not a public inquiry should be held. This may be a full inquiry considering all aspects of the development, or a local planning inquiry which is limited to the narrower local implications. Even this remains outside local control, since the recommendations of the inquiry reporter (a senior civil servant accountable to the Secretary of State) can be rejected by the Scottish Secretary and the development approved regardless.

The history of the opposition to the NATO expansion at Stornoway airport shows how the planning inquiry system is loaded against objectors. The initial approach to Comhairle nan Eilean (the Western Isles Council) by the MOD in 1977 to lengthen the runway, build aircraft parking areas, new fuel tanks and other facilities, was treated by the council very much like any other planning application. It was approved on condition that the effects on civil aviation, recreation and ecology and the routing of construction traffic should be further discussed; that land should be reinstated after pipeline construction, and that excavation of the sand spit at the north end of the runway should be avoided since it is a Site of Special Scientific Interest (SSSI). The council asked that construction workers be locally recruited, night flying kept to a minimum and sound-proofing offered to local residents.

Strong local objections forced the council to reverse their decision in 1978. In the meantime the MOD was 'reconsidering' its plans – expanding them from a £6 million scheme in 1977 to £20 million by March 1980 and £40 million by May 1980. In the face of the council's opposition the MOD referred their plans to the Secretary of State for Scotland, and after much delay a local planning inquiry was called. This was limited to purely planning matters. The MOD's rationale for proposing a NATO base at Stornoway was not to be considered.

The inquiry reporter, a supposedly neutral chairman, arrived for the inquiry aboard the same RAF VIP plane which carried the RAF's high-powered public relations delegation. No NATO witnesses were present and the entire military case was presented as a purely RAF one in an attempt to dispel local fears of Stornoway becoming a foreign military base. The lead military witness, Air Marshal Peter Bairsto, spent some time outlining the strategic need for military expansion at Stornoway, and the nature of the Soviet threat – both of which were impermissible evidence outside the inquiry remit – without challenge from the reporter. RAF witnesses stated that they could not comment on possible use by other NATO members despite the fact that the entire development is NATO-funded and for NATO use.

Comhairle nan Eilean's evidence on likely noise disturbance was accepted by the reporter. The disturbance would be unacceptable, and on that basis, he stated, there should be a presumption against the development. But in a complete evasion of his responsibilities the reporter concluded that 'the planning presumption against the development . . . can only be overcome by convincing evidence of a need [for a military base] that cannot be met elsewhere', but 'complete evidence on that point was not led at the inquiry and I therefore feel unable to make any recommendation.'[22] In other words, he could not follow through his own belief in the planning arguments against the base because he had insufficient information on the strategic arguments which his own inquiry was forbidden to discuss. This left the way open for the Secretary of State to give the go-ahead for the base on 1 December 1981 by ignoring the planning arguments and stating that national security required a base at Stornoway. The opposition case had, on the admission of the inquiry reporter, succeeding in demonstrating that had this been a private planning application it would have been refused. By limiting the terms of the inquiry the government had turned the exercise into a sham.

The military have also been taking it upon themselves to act as ultimate planning authority in some places. The introduction of a new combined fuel and explosives supply ship in NATO has created new safety zoning requirements round the NATO POL depots at Campbeltown and Aultbea. The MOD has told the local authorities there that they wish to see all planning applications relating to sites within a given distance of the POL installations.

At the same time the military are exempt from many planning laws. Neither SDD Circular 23/73 nor the Control of Pollution Act 1974 can be used to control the noise caused by military aircraft. Nor are nuclear submarine bases such as Faslane and Rosyth subject to the laws on the discharge of radioactive waste into the sea. The Scottish experience certainly supports one planner's view that 'the need for a national defence system tends to run contrary to the needs of good planning in rural areas.'[23]

Tourism and the military wilderness

Tourist advertising has helped to perpetuate the image of Scotland as one of the last unspoilt wildernesses of Europe. Uist has been described as 'a sprawling, isolated community, sustained by sheep, whisky, Gaelic pride and awesome scenery';[24] the seas and lochs around the Scottish coast are 'Europe's finest, most unspoiled waters.'[25]

The reality behind these images reflects the social and economic history of Scotland, particularly the Highlands and Islands – generations of depopulation, the maintenance of large tracts of land purely for deer and grouse, and longstanding difficulties in developing either indigenous or external economic investment.

However, the perpetuation of the wilderness image has another facet – the interests of the military in maintaining a large sparsely-populated area within the UK for training purposes. The strong link between the tourist image and military requirements is seen in sharp focus in the case of low-flying American pilots, and low-level sightseeing is responsible for regular breaches of what few restrictions there are on low-flying. The existence of a large depopulated area in north-west Scotland was the reason for the establishment of the Highlands Restricted Area there. Similarly the continued existence of large tracts of hill land such as Cape Wrath, Garelochhead, Tighnablair and Auchallater for use as military training areas depends on their lack of economic development except for limited agricultural purposes and as 'unspoilt' scenery for tourists.

In other places the eyesore of military developments and the adverse impact of military activity on tourism have led to opposition from conservation and tourist bodies and local authorities. Following many years of naval and air bombardment of the area around Cape Wrath, which have resulted in shrapnel injuries to a local woman, near misses to several fishing boats, damage to buildings in the area and the deaths of many sheep and which have adversely affected tourism, the Highland Regional Council took the bold step of adopting the closure of the Cape Wrath ranges as part of their planning policy. The text of the 1980 *North-West Sutherland Local Plan* reads : 'The Regional Council consider that the naval bombardment range at Cape Wrath is a constraint to tourist development in the area and would welcome discussions with the Ministry of Defence with a view to their ceasing use of the site.'[26] Tourists and the military may seek the same thing in the Highland landscape, but their activities are evidently far from compatible.

In the Lothians, a long fight between the regional and district councils and the MOD over a proposed new army firing range at Castlelaw on the south side of the Pentlands culminated in the Secretary of State for Scotland approving the range despite strong evidence in the public inquiry of its detrimental effect on the increasing use of the Pentland Hills for recreational purposes. As with the Stornoway inquiry decision later in 1981, the go-ahead was given in spite of the substance of the inquiry report, and citing 'overriding national considerations' as the justification. In north Aberdeenshire, where the landscape for many miles around is dominated by Mormond Hill and its dozens of enormous tropospheric scatter aerials, the conservation group 'Keep Grampian Beautiful' has criticised the junkyard appearance of the hill and the progressive encroachment of military and oil-related radio stations on parts of the hill of conservation value.

In some areas where acquiescence to rampant military expansion and the presence of nuclear weapons is well established, local tourist authorities are even attempting to attract holidaymakers to the military establishments in the area. Kintyre CND came up with the following delightful quote from a tourist brochure in Campbeltown in 1982:

> Also at Campbeltown is a NATO base where sea-going warlike vessels fill up with fuel, and, two or three miles from the town, an RAF airfield with one of the longest runways in Europe. What with frigates, minesweepers, nuclear submarines and the latest aircraft there is plenty for the mechanically-minded to see, as opposed to those who prefer the beauties of landscapes, Highland cattle and seashore sights . . . Kintyre, in fact, has just about everything.[27]

One suspects that the prospect of throngs of 'mechanically-minded' holidaymakers sightseeing round the US navy nuclear weapons store at Machrihanish would not be looked on kindly by the military police.

The campaign for hearts and minds

Public support for a large and expanding military establishment is heavily dependent on the projection of an image of caring, community-minded armed forces whose peacetime role is not primarily preparation for war but support for local charities and community organisations. The creation of this image takes up a large percentage of the time and effort of military community relations officers and high-level staff throughout the armed forces.

The Americans have led the way in this field, but local people in Sandbank and Dunoon have some problems in being convinced that the considerable increase in crime levels and chemical and nuclear pollution since the US navy dropped anchor in the Holy Loch are a good thing. The base commander used 'a number of thinly disguised inducements to help sway local opinion' in favour of the renewed expansion of shore facilities in 1982–83. He appeared to believe that the US navy has a peculiar right and ability to persuade the BBC and local authorities to provide improved TV reception and community facilities in the area.[28]

At Edzell, when the National Security Agency cryptologists are not tapping international communications, they are, we are told, making 'outstanding efforts in furthering cordial community relations in the UK and strengthening the Scottish–American alliance', for which they received the US Ambassador's Award in the mid-1970s.[29]

The smokescreen of community relations is also a well-established tactic of the British military. Awards to units for their community work and charity fund-raising are numerous, the main one being the Wilkinson Sword of Peace. In 1980 this was awarded to 112 Signals Unit, RAF Stornoway, who had raised funds for many worthy causes in Lewis. So effective was this façade of good works that the RAF managed to prevent even those opposed to the NATO expansion at Stornoway from discovering that 112 Signals Unit's role for the many years it operated at Stornoway had been to assist Vulcan bomber crews to use Stornoway and other places in the Western Isles as simulated targets for nuclear bombs.

Operation Military Aid to the Civil Community (OPMACC) started in Scotland in 1966–67. This incorporates everything from charity activity, through mountain and air–sea rescue operations and bomb disposal, to the construction of airstrips and footbridges by Royal Engineers. All these activities are designed to fulfil the dual requirements of establishing the image of the military as a useful member of the community and giving the services useful training which is not available within the military establishment.

Some OPMACC activities – notably the rescue services – are undoubtedly of great benefit to the community. Their purpose, however, is by no means selfless. The same helicopters which provide rescue cover from Prestwick have a nuclear anti-submarine capability, while RAF rescue helicopters would not be present in Scotland were it not for the scale of RAF flying, since their primary mission is the rescue of military personnel. OPMACC has built several airstrips in the Highlands since 1968. All of these now form useful parts of the military infrastructure, and although a number of organisations have asked the army to build cheap grass airstrips for local communities, they have refused since only hard surface strips are of use in construction training or for subsequent military activity.

The cultural conflict

The cultural impact of military bases is most evident in the case of installations where a large, shifting population, mostly of single men, is imposed on a small town or rural area.

Balivanich, the domestic and administrative headquarters of the Royal Artillery missile range on South Uist, now constitutes a small town, with rows of army houses, a NAAFI supermarket and a population of non-Gaelic speaking, predominantly English military personnel and their dependants – a marked contrast to even 15 years ago when Balivanich was still largely a crofting township with minor developments around the airport. The impact of such a population, most of whom stay in the Uists for two years or less, is considerable. One particular problem arises in education: the Western Isles Council's efforts to re-establish Gaelic as the teaching language are thwarted by the army's presence in Benbecula.

Perhaps the most noticeable effect on local culture is the impact of a large military male presence on local young women. Round most of the larger bases, many local women find themselves marrying sailors, soldiers or airmen. Sexual attacks are often more prevalent in these areas. Competition between servicemen and local males has been known to spill over into violence. The army in the Uists do not permit locals to attend their fortnightly dances because of fear of fights, although there is no restriction on service personnel attending local dances. In November 1981 these tensions led to a bus containing visiting personnel of an RAF Rapier missile squadron from Germany being stoned by locals after fights broke out at a dance at Iochdar. Street fighting has also occurred from time to time with US navy personnel in Dunoon and Campbeltown. In October 1982 a race riot broke out amongst sailors on the USS *Hunley* in the Holy Loch.

The impact of military bases and activities, whether at local or national level, depends on the degree to which the armed forces are culturally distinct from the rest of society. John Nott's boost to the TAVR and the creation of a new 'Dad's Army', the Home Service Force, in 1982, could be seen as an attempt to break down this distinction at a time when mass unemployment is causing many young people to be disaffected from both society and the military. While a conventional defence force closely integrated with society is no bad thing in principle, the attempts to do this in Britain now cannot be divorced from the existing organisation of the armed forces as a professional, high technology, nuclear-equipped force. All reserve units are closely integrated with regular forces and nuclear training is a standard part of their activity. An increasing proportion of TAVR units are being allocated to the role of reinforcing the British army of the Rhine in Germany, and the 23 per cent increase in TAVR strength to 86,000 by the early 1990s also permits more territorials to take on a home defence task which, as 'civil defence' exercises have shown, consists largely of rounding up wayward members of the public during the run-up to nuclear war. Strengthened reserves are not intended to reduce the social and cultural gaps between the civil and military populations. They are yet another element in the evolving strategy for fighting a nuclear war in Europe.

4. Directory of bases

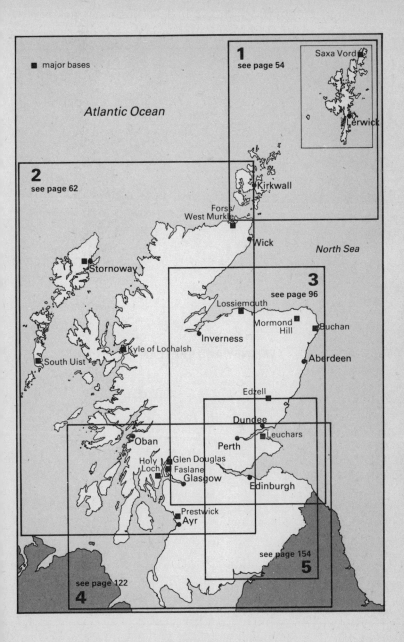

■ major bases

Atlantic Ocean

1
see page 54

Saxa Vord ■

Lerwick ■

2
see page 62

Kirkwall

Forss/
West Murkle

Wick

North Sea

Stornoway

3
see page 96

Lossiemouth

Mormond
Hill

Buchan

Inverness

Aberdeen

Kyle of Lochalsh

South Uist

Edzell

Dundee

Oban

Perth

Leuchars

Holy
Loch

Glen Douglas

Faslane
Glasgow

Edinburgh

Prestwick
Ayr

see page 154

5

see page 122

4

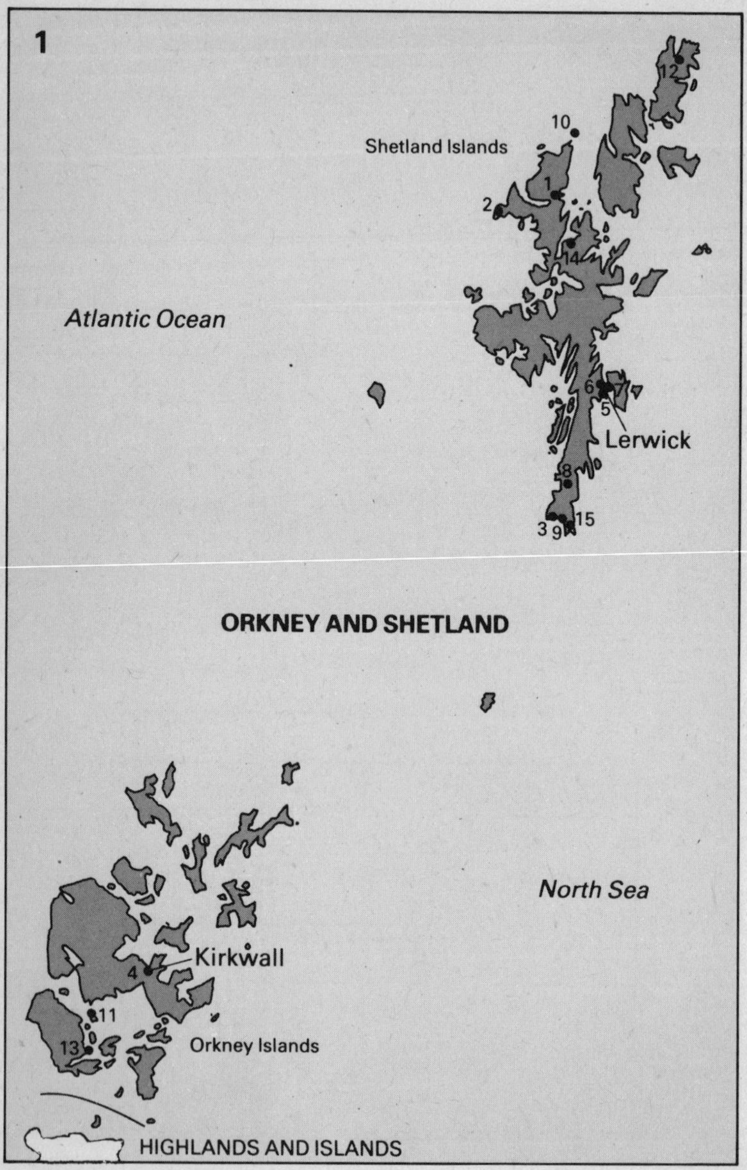

1

Shetland Islands

10

2

14

Atlantic Ocean

6
5
Lerwick

8

3 9 15

ORKNEY AND SHETLAND

North Sea

Kirkwall

4

11

13

Orkney Islands

HIGHLANDS AND ISLANDS

Section one: Orkney and Shetland

1. Collafirth Hill, Shetland 'Shetlands Relay' station in the NATO ACE HIGH communications system. Microwave radio dishes on a tall mast provide the link between Saxa Vord and Mossy Hill.

2. Esha Ness, Shetland Listed in official documents as an RN station;[1] its function is unknown and it may now be disused.

3. Garths Ness, Sumburgh, Shetland RAF communications station; precise function unknown.

4. Kirkwall, Orkney Territorial Army (TAVR) infantry, A Company, 2nd Battalion 51st Highland Volunteers.

5. Lerwick, Shetland Major weather station operated by the Meteorological Office, which is part of the MOD. Besides its everyday civilian applications and its importance to civil and military air operations, knowledge of environmental conditions is essential to the performance of radar systems and sonar equipment, command and control, anti-submarine warfare and the aiming of ballistic missile warheads. The geographical location of this weather station, its radiosonde facilities for upper atmosphere sampling, and the proximity of ocean weather buoys off Yell give it a special military significance, and data from here is likely to be used by a wide variety of NATO and US forces. Meteorological data from here is also fed into the Royal Observer Corps (ROC) network for nuclear fall-out prediction.

6. Lerwick, Shetland TAVR infantry, one platoon of A Company, 2nd Battalion 51st Highland Volunteers.

7. Lerwick Harbour, Shetland Naval port HQ. Regularly visited by NATO vessels, particularly diesel submarines tasked to 'barrier' patrols in the Iceland–UK gap, during NATO maritime exercises.

8. Mossy Hill, Shetland NATO ACE HIGH communications station run by the army's Signal Corps. The station was completed in 1961 and has microwave radio links to Saxa Vord via Collafirth Hill, and troposcatter links to Mormond Hill, Sola in Norway and the Faeroe Islands. The latter link is believed to connect a NATO/Danish radar station on Stremoy to ACE HIGH and/or the UK Air Defence Ground Environment (UKADGE).

9. Quendale, Sumburgh, Shetland TAVR small-arms firing range.

10. Ramna Stacks, Shetland A group of skerries at the head of Yell Sound used in the past as a ship-to-shore gunnery target area by the Royal Navy. Its present status is unknown.

11. Ramsdale, Orkney TAVR small-arms firing range.

12. Saxa Vord, Unst, Shetland RAF radar station, originally part of the 'ROTOR' and 'Linesman' systems and later an early-warning outpost subordinate to the Buchan Sector Operations Centre. It also served as a standby control centre, capable of independent operation if necessary. Saxa Vord remains under the control of Buchan in the new updated UKADGE (UK Air Defence Ground Environment) but the revised philosophy of centralised command and decentralised control makes Saxa Vord much more capable of autonomous operation and control of air defence forces.

In a £10 million NATO-funded project, a new Marconi s649 surveillance radar and a related HF200 height-finding radar were installed and became operational here in June 1979. Both radars are enclosed in weatherproof green 'golfball' radomes. The s649 provides data on aircraft at ranges of 200 miles and up to 100,000 feet altitude – i.e. as far as the Faeroes or the Norwegian coast. Both radars have anti-jamming capabilities.

Saxa Vord can pass surveillance, command and control data to other UKADGE and NADGE (NATO Air Defence Ground Environment) stations in the UK, Norway and Faeroes by various communications links. Since 1979 Saxa Vord appears to have received a satellite communications terminal to provide a new 'redundant' data path to other suitably equipped sites, probably via NATO satellites, the UK's 'Skynet' or the US DSCS (Defense Satellite Communications System). This terminal was probably installed as part of the NAEGIS (NATO Airborne Early Warning Ground Integration Segment) project, under which Saxa Vord will be able to transmit and receive data from and to Nimrod AEW.3 and E-3 AWACS aircraft and relay it to other parts of the network. Saxa Vord is also part of ACE HIGH, with a microwave link to Collafirth Hill feeding data from here into the NATO communications system.

Saxa Vord's importance has increased with the advent of NAEGIS; the station will work closely with NATO Airborne Early Warning aircraft, relaying data between these, its own or other NADGE radars, ships and other aircraft, and shore command centres. It could monitor long-range strike aircraft en route to attack Soviet naval forces or installations around the Kola Peninsula.

Although the RAF likes to present Saxa Vord's role as one of warding off droves of 'Russian bombers', the base's personnel do not seem to be overburdened with this task. They find time to operate a number of primarily non-military facilities, and indeed there are so few Soviet aircraft for them to track and intercept that the station's fighter controllers get out of practice. They require about 40 interceptions a month to 'keep their hand in', but in the first six months of 1982 Saxa Vord handled fewer than 30 interceptions, or just over one a week – much lower than the usual figures bandied about by the MOD.[2] To compensate, the RAF has installed an electronic simulator at Saxa Vord.

Saxa Vord is also likely to record details of the electronic emissions from the Soviet aircraft which it tracks – i.e. an electronic intelligence (ELINT) function. The RAF's 91 Signals Unit is also based at Saxa Vord, and may perform this ELINT task, or operate other communications facilities such as Defence Communications Network (DCN), Strike Command Integrated Communication System (STCICS) or MATELO. There are 187 RAF personnel at Saxa Vord, and although there have been suggestions that this station might operate part of the US SOSUS (Sound Surveillance System) undersea hydrophone network, this would be an insufficient number for such a task.

Other facilities at Saxa Vord are the Shetland Radar Advisory Service, instituted in 1978 to reduce the risk of collision between oil-related helicopters and low-flying military aircraft in the area; an RAF TACAN radio navigation beacon; a National Air Traffic Services (NATS) VHF/UHF radio relay for civil and military air traffic control, and the RAF-run Norwick Radio, which provides HF radio links with offshore oil installations. The latter could also be of use to the RAF.

The military potential of North Sea oil rigs

As early as 1975, the potential of offshore oil installations for military tasks was being discussed.[3] Many of the troposcatter and other radio links from the mainland and Shetland to offshore installations could provide a very useful communications infrastructure for any such military use, either as communications relays in their own right or for transmitting data from anti-submarine, air defence radar or electronic warfare sensors placed on the rigs themselves. The government was being urged in 1975 to put Rapier anti-aircraft missiles on oil rigs, ostensibly for self-protection but with obvious potential as a forward line of defence for the many military targets in the UK. That the government has plans to use oil rigs in an offensive role became clear in 1982, during one of the triennial 'Mallet Blow' tactical air exercises. The exercise involved over 120 sorties a day by USAF and RAF strike/attack aircraft against simulated Soviet targets on the Otterburn and Spadeadam ranges in northern England. For the duration of the exercise the RAF took over the Rough Field gas platform off the Humber estuary for use as an Air Support Operations Centre (ASOC) by the RAF's 38 Group Tactical Communications Wing (TCW). The TCW's role was to radio target information to attack aircraft as they flew up the North Sea to Otterburn. The exercise demonstrated the military's ability to take over oil rigs behind enemy lines (as 'Rough' was in the exercise scenario), rapidly deploy an RAF TCW to an offshore installation, potential or actual takeover of British Telecom's offshore microwave radio circuits and operation of these under jamming conditions. Such use of oil platforms would be particularly relevant to NATO attacks on Soviet targets in and around the Kola Peninsula, and it is notable that several military units assigned to north Norway took part in the exercise.

Since 1975 there have been a number of Soviet air and sea incursions into the 500 metre safety zones of North Sea oil rigs, and it is apparent that the USSR is increasingly concerned about the possible NATO use of Western offshore oil installations which are moving steadily closer to Soviet strategic waters.

13. Scapa Flow, Orkney This sheltered body of water has been used as a naval anchorage for over 70 years. The RN shore base closed in 1957 and the Lyness naval fuel depot on Hoy was dismantled in 1978–79, but it seems that Scapa Flow is kept on a care and maintenance basis. During the NATO maritime exercise 'Ocean Safari' in 1981, Scapa became a naval port HQ manned by personnel from Pitreavie; the anchorage was used by, amongst others, US naval vessels of classes which carry Terrier and ASROC nuclear weapons. In May 1983 the anchorage was used by the new RN anti-submarine warfare (ASW) carrier HMS *Illustrious*.

14. Scatsta, Shetland Located on the south shore of Sullom Voe; site of a US Coast Guard Loran-C monitor station in the Norwegian Sea chain of that system. The base was commissioned in 1967 and works with a master station in the Faeroes and other 'slaves' on Jan Mayen Island, Bo in Norway and Sylt in West Germany. The Loran-C LF navigation system was built as the principal source of US SSBN navigational data in the northern hemisphere but it is also available to civilian navigators. Scatsta's job is to ensure stable interstation synchronisation which is crucial to the accuracy of the SSBNs' inertial navigation system and hence to the eventual accuracy of Poseidon warheads. It also increases the patrol areas in which Loran-C is effective. Under the Clarinet Pilgrim programme, Loran-C stations have been equipped to broadcast command and control messages, such as launch orders, to SSBNs.

The US Coast Guard (USCG) is part of the US navy in wartime but otherwise it is part of the US Department of Transportation. Scatsta has 17 USCG and 5 civilian staff who live beside the airfield. The monitor station itself is located at the end of a disused runway. The base keeps in touch with the other Loran-C stations by HF radio. The USCG's sole EC-130E Hercules visits Sumburgh airfield occasionally; the runway at Scatsta is not strong enough to accept this aircraft when it is loaded. The Hercules probably does checking and calibration work on Loran-C though it may also bring in equipment and supplies for Scatsta.

There are local rumours that this station will close as soon as the USCG can find a site to relocate it in an automated form. Presumably the new site will also be in Shetland and it will be interesting to see if the USA uses that opportunity to add any other facilities.

There is no evidence to support the suggestions that Scatsta houses the UK terminal of the Greenland–Iceland–UK gap SOSUS anti-submarine surveillance chain.

15. Sumburgh Airport, Shetland The rapid decline in oil-related civil air traffic here prompted one official of Shetland Islands Council to approach the MOD in March 1981, during the NATO base public inquiry at Stornoway, suggesting Sumburgh as an alternative for NATO expansion. The airport is already used by military helicopters en route to NATO exercises in Norway and it was very heavily used during the NATO invasion of Shetland in exercise 'Northern Wedding' in 1978. The MOD may have its eye on Sumburgh's military potential. In 1980 a prominent strategist stated that 'a possible alternative [to expanding US bases in Iceland and Greenland] would be to establish a new NATO base on some British-owned site either in Britain itself or in the island area north of Scotland.'[4]

Near the airport are two 'civil' radars which were 30 per cent funded by the MOD – a Marconi s1061 primary radar, installed on Sumburgh Head in 1979, and a Cossor secondary surveillance radar which became operational on Fitful Head in 1980. Both have signal characteristics compatible with UKADGE and are of direct use in extending military radar coverage.

Section two: the Highlands and Islands

16. Achtascailt, Dundonnell Former youth hostel bought by the MOD in 1977 and now used as an Army Mountain Training Centre.

17. Aird Uig, Lewis RAF HF radio station, believed to be part of the 'Flight Watch' system, providing communications with RAF (and probably other NATO) transport aircraft over the North Atlantic, therefore an important element in the control of the US military reinforcement of Europe. Aird Uig has a 250 ft transmitter mast and a smaller receiver/DF aerial. The station is operated by personnel from RAF Stornoway and has been in use since the late 1960s.

18. Alness, Easter Ross Base of 1100 Marine Craft Unit RAF which operates the Long Range Recovery and Support Craft (LRRSCS) *Seal* and *Seagull* (used for target-towing for RAF Nimrods and other aircraft, weapons and sonobuoy recovery, and co-operation with RN units during exercises off Scotland), a 42 ft range safety launch (used as a platform for dinghy drills and helicopter winching exercises during aircrew sea-survival training) and a Gemini inflatable which is occasionally used by bomb disposal teams at Cape Wrath range. There are 85 personnel at Alness and the MOD owns 34 houses in the town. The unit's vessels are berthed at the naval pier at Invergordon.

19. Aultbea, Wester Ross NATO Petroleum, Oil annd Lubricants (POL) Depot, built in 1966 to refuel Royal Fleet Auxiliaries and other military tankers and warships, mainly during NATO naval exercises off the north of Scotland. Aultbea was built as a wartime facility; the funds used in its construction are solely for wartime operational facilities. Heavy fuel oil is stored in underground tanks in a 200 acre area behind the pier, with stocks being removed every few months to refineries in Holland and Spain for recycling. In 1981, due to future use of Aultbea by combined fuel and explosives supply ships (AORS), the MOD announced it wanted to ban all construction or new development within 900 metres of the NATO pier and to have right of veto over any developments within 2.3 km (encompassing the whole of Aultbea village), due to an enlarged safety zone

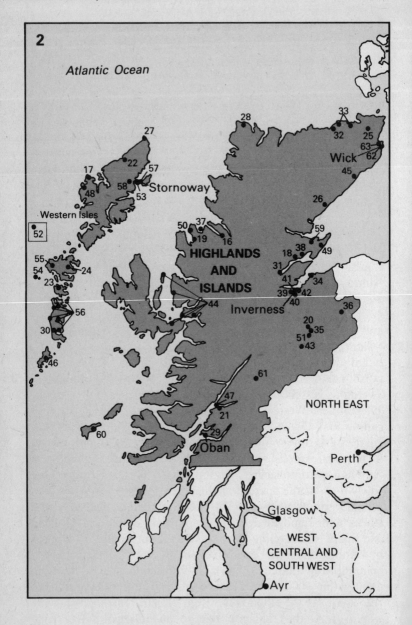

2

Atlantic Ocean

28

33

27

32

25

63

Wick

62

17

22

57

45

58

Stornoway

53

26

Western Isles

50 37

59

52

19 16

18 38

49

HIGHLANDS

55

AND

31

54

24

ISLANDS

41 34

23

39 42

40

56

44 Inverness

36

30

20 35

51

43

46

61

NORTH EAST

47

21

60

29

Oban

Perth

Glasgow

WEST
CENTRAL AND
SOUTH WEST

Ayr

because of the increased danger of an explosion. The new vessels are expected to visit Aultbea about nine times a year. The district council opposed the ban and in early 1983 was seeking MOD assurances that no ammunition would be dumped ashore, safeguarding zones would not be further enlarged, onshore oil developments would not be opposed by the MOD, and nuclear weapons would never be stored at Aultbea. In fact there is no weapons storage area here, but following revelations during the Falklands war about habitual carriage of nuclear weapons aboard RN ships it is likely that ships with these weapons on board use Aultbea's facilities. The depot employs 20 civilians.

20. Badaguish, Aviemore RAF Mountain Training Centre, bought in 1983.

21. Ballachulish, Argyll Joint Services Mountain Training Centre.

22. Barvas, Lewis TAVR small-arms firing range.

23. Benbecula, Western Isles

(a) RAF radar station on Balivanich airfield, established 1972, officially to detect Soviet 'backdoor' attacks from the north-west. The station has a semi-mobile Marconi Type 88/89 radar system which could in theory be moved to pre-surveyed dispersal sites in time of tension or war; however the equipment at Benbecula was installed as a 'gap-filler' and its mobility is not utilised.

Benbecula is a Control and Reporting Centre (CRC) which feeds radar information to the Sector Operations Centre (SOC) at Buchan; at present the data are transmitted by landline, but the multi-billion pound UKADGE update will add live video transmissions by narrowband microwave, tropospheric scatter and satellite communications. Benbecula's role is to detect, identify and track aircraft up to 200 nautical miles to the west and north-west; any aircraft which cannot be identified from civil flight plans or by IFF interrogation are reported through Buchan; fighters, usually RAF Phantoms from Leuchars, are sent out to intercept and identify the radar contact. Most of these interceptions are Soviet maritime patrol aircraft – usually Bear-DS or -FS or Badgers which, despite the regular propaganda about bombers probing our airspace, are actually 'going about their lawful business over international waters',[5] usually in transit from bases near Murmansk to their operational areas in mid-Atlantic. These interceptions are so few that, as noted under Saxa Vord, most radar controllers are receiving insufficient interception training to keep them up to operational standard. This problem is overcome by using RAF and USAF aircraft – Buccaneers, F-111s, Phantoms, Hawks, Canberras, Jaguars and Tornados – to perform mock attacks on the airfield, the radar picture being recorded on videotape for further analysis and future training. A further development of this practice occurred in mid-April 1982 when RAF Vulcans were adapted from a nuclear to a conventional bombing role for the Falklands war. The training for the attacks on Port Stanley airfield was carried out by Vulcans making simulated attacks on Benbecula. (Evidently they did not train hard enough since the raids failed.)

Despite MOD persistence with the notion of the Soviet bomber threat from the north-west, the scenarios of the major air defence exercises in Britain in recent years have omitted these 'back door' attacks. This is because 'the RAF seem assured that this area will be adequately covered by the Nimrod AEW.3 force operating in concert with the NATO E-3A Sentry AWACS units'[6] – in other words any Soviet threat from the north-west would be countered many hundreds of miles offshore, well beyond the range of shore-based radar. The function of Benbecula is more accurately described by Wood, who states that the capacity of the new UKADGE network 'has to be such that it is able to cope with the massive influx of US combat aircraft into the UK in times of tension or war.'[7] A microwave link from the existing RAF radar station to the Army Range Control Building on Rueval, South Uist, suggests that a secondary function of RAF Benbecula is to transmit data on aircraft infringing the range danger area to Range Control, complementing the army's own missile tracking and sea-watch radars.

As part of the massive revamping of UKADGE the MOD applied to Comhairle nan Eilean in 1976 for their comments on a plan to erect a completely new radar station, with a 50 ft high radome and a fully-hardened underground command and control building, adjacent to the army missile tracking radar on the summit of South Clettraval (see below). Following objections on amenity grounds the MOD agreed to split their new radar station, with the radars remaining on Clettraval but the control building and associated facilities to be located at East Camp, Balivanich – across the airfield from the current radar station. Construction at the Clettraval site began in August 1981 and at the East Camp site in summer 1982; both are scheduled for completion in 1983 but by October 1982 the S-band radar to be installed at Clettraval had still not been ordered, following a series of delays and disputes in the NATO-funded purchase of three such radars for UKADGE. The new radar station is unlikely to be operational before 1985.

In 1978 there were 60 RAF personnel at Benbecula; this figure is likely to increase substantially when the new UKADGE radar station comes into service, adding further to the domination of life in the Uists by the military.

(b) Balivanich airfield itself is used by RAF Hercules transport aircraft to move army and RAF Regiment missile units from bases in Germany and Britain to the South Uist missile range for two-week missile practice camps. Missiles, equipment and personnel are all flown into Balivanich, with an average of about three Hercules flights a week. Military aircraft account for about 13 per cent of total traffic at Benbecula airfield, a higher proportion than virtually all other civil airfields in Scotland, and complete military takeover of the airfield (as occurred for 11 months in 1957–58 during construction of the missile range) is a distinct possibility when the new radar station is operational, particularly when NATO expansion at both Stornoway and Uist is complete. The MOD spent £2 million strengthening the runway in 1977 to take fully-loaded Hercules. The airfield is insufficiently equipped to handle the RAF Canberras which tow targets at the missile range, but in June 1982 officers from the RAF's advanced flying school at Valley in Anglesey inspected the airfield for possible use by that unit's Hawk jets for flying training detachments.

If the Greek government closes the NATO Missile Firing

Installation (NAMFI) in Crete, the US army are almost certain to move their missile firing activities to Benbecula; in this event Benbecula airfield will be expanded to accommodate USAF C-141 and C-5 transport planes. Other military use of the airfield includes regular overshoots and mock attacks by a wide variety of aircraft including Jaguars, Phantoms, Canberras and Hawks, and visits by trials establishment and arms company aircraft in connection with the missile range. Benbecula would play an important role, like Stornoway, in the US air reinforcement of Europe.

(c) Administrative and domestic headquarters, Royal Artillery Guided Weapons Range, Hebrides. A large complex of buildings has developed from the original small establishment in 1959. The main building was completed in 1974, and married quarters for most of the 370 military personnel built nearby between 1971 and 1978, all part of a major expansion programme from 1968 onwards at a total cost of some £20 million. The military and their dependants now make up about 50 per cent of the population of Benbecula. The operational side of the missile range is centred on South Uist (see below).

24. Blashaval, North Uist In July 1982 the Western Isles Council was told by the MOD that they intended to erect a tower and other equipment on this hill for wind-flow experiments. This is thought to be in connection with the new radar station on Clettraval.

25. Bower, Caithness Composite Signals Organisation Station, part of the government's spying network. Bower's days as a SIGINT station seem to be at an end since the site was sold in 1980 to make room for radio aerials associated with 'Project Sabre', a joint UK–West German five-year investigation of the aurora borealis (Northern Lights). This is likely to be of considerable interest to the military in improving the propagation of radio and radar signals in polar regions.

26. Brora, Sutherland Composite Signals Organisation Station. The HF direction-finding equipment here is engaged in eavesdropping on Warsaw Pact and probably other countries' radio messages. It previously operated in conjunction with Bower. Brora is due to close in 1986; the 50 staff will be transferred elsewhere in the GCHQ establishment. Press reports in 1981 suggested that Brora tracks Soviet spy satellites but there are no suitable aerials there for such a task.

Brora's American Free Church minister has said that if Brora became a Soviet target in war it would not be because of the CSO station but because of the sins of the people – 'it would be retributive justice.'[8]

27. Butt of Lewis Lighthouse, Western Isles The Admiralty Surface Weapons Establishment, responsible for developing naval communications equipment, had a small radio aerial here in the late 1970s. This was said to be an experimental VLF receiver but its size makes this doubtful. Its present status is unknown.

28. Cape Wrath, Sutherland An 8,308 acre RN and RAF weapons range and army exercise area. The two weapons ranges are:

(a) A ship-to-shore bombardment range, originally established in the 1930s. Cape Wrath is now the only ship-to-shore bombardment range in Europe. Ships of the RN and other NATO (and occasionally non-NATO) navies use the range for practice firing of their 4.5 inch and 5 inch guns at car wrecks up to two miles inland. The cliffs are used as ranging marks for the guns, and torpedoes and rockets are also fired at the cliffs or offshore. From a level of use of five or six days a month in 1976 the naval bombardment range activity has now expanded to up to 14 days a month despite a decline in the number of gun-equipped ships. Sheep are regularly killed or maimed by the bombardments, and in 1968 Mrs Nellie Munro of Durness was injured by shrapnel from an off-target shell while collecting cockles on the shore of the Kyle of Durness. More recently a marine went missing without trace while on exercise on the range and a holidaymaker also disappeared without trace while camping in the area. The MOD said the disappearances were unconnected with range firing. In 1978 two lobster boats narrowly escaped being blown out of the water by three frigates when firing started as they were picking up creels just offshore.

The inland part of the range, as well as being a target area for naval guns, is regularly used for army and marines exercises, including the firing of small arms and guns of all sizes. The tourist road to Cape Wrath lighthouse runs right through the middle of the range.

(b) An Garbh-eilean (Garvie Island) an air bombardment range, one of the few in Europe available for live dropping of 1,000 lb bombs. Used mainly by RAF Jaguars (including those based in Germany) and, since the Falklands war, RAF Vulcans adapted for conventional bombing. Future heavy use by RAF Tornados is likely, and other NATO air forces also use the range, notably USAF F-111s. A sergeant from the 48th TFW at Lakenheath recently described these operations: 'They go up there, bomb the shit out of some little island off the coast of Scotland, using smoke bombs, you know. I've seen the pictures. It's really neat.'[9]

A maximum of forty-eight 1,000 lb bombs can be dropped on the island in any one month, and rocket and cannon firing is also permitted. This means that, since Garvie Island range cannot be used at the same time as naval bombardment is going on, and bombing and shelling does not normally take place at weekends, there is virtually continuous use of the Cape Wrath ranges on weekdays.

Garvie Island has been used for aerial bombardment since the 1950s. Several aircraft en route to the range have had to jettison their bombs or have crashed with live weapons on board. The most recent was an RAF Jaguar which crashed on a hill behind Brora in September 1982. In October 1979 one of the same lobster boats which had been shelled by frigates 11 months previously narrowly escaped damage when picking up creels off Garvie Island during a period of range inactivity. A bomb disposal team detonated five unexploded 1,000 lb bombs on the island, showering the sea around with shrapnel and rock debris. The boat's skipper, Gordon Bain, estimated that there were 500 unexploded bombs in the sea off Cape Wrath.

Bombing and shelling at Cape Wrath can be heard 35 miles away at Bettyhill, and local houses have suffered structural damage from vibration. Local councillors have also expressed concern at the impact on tourism and in 1980 succeeded in getting the Highland Regional Council to adopt a policy of scaling down activity at the range with a view to its eventual closure, although this is outside the council's jurisdiction. The MOD responded by stating that they were negotiating a new 21 year lease on the range and would use a compulsory purchase' order if necessary. Following the near-disastrous incidents with fishing boats in 1978–79, the MOD has proposed a new set of bye-laws prohibiting access to the range area (which extends 25 miles offshore and up to 55,000 feet), but only in 1980 was radio equipment installed at the range control hut to enable range controllers to contact fishing boats in the area; not all of the range area is visible from the control hut, yet there is no radar to ensure that the range is clear; nor are there any range safety or patrol boats. The range control hut is on Faraid Head.

29. Connel, Oban Built in 1961–62 as HQ 27 Group Royal Observer Corps (ROC), controlling 40 ROC monitoring posts between Mallaig and the Clyde. In April 1973, 27 Group was disbanded and Connel's functions transferred to Inverness and Prestwick. Connel then became a communications centre under 30 Group ROC (Inverness) to which it is linked by landline. No other ROC group has a separate communications centre, suggesting that Connel has a special function. This was confirmed at an open night at an ROC HQ in Scotland in 1982, when ROC personnel stated that Connel was jointly run by the navy, army, air force and ROC, and was not part of the established ROC/ UKWMO warning network.

Connel is thought to be an important element in the US INCA (Integrated Nuclear Communications Assessment) system, which 'involves the assessment of VLF, LF, HF and VHF/UHF radio links for the National Command Authorities to European Theatre; for benign, as well as nuclear and ECM stressed conditions . . . The programme also includes analysis of Atlantic, Mediterranean and English Channel submarine cables.'[10] It is probably no coincidence that Connel was the eastern landfall of the first NATO transatlantic cable, TAT 1, and the CANTAT cable from Canada. Connel is also close to the British Telecom (BT) trunkline network, with lines to Glasgow, Lochgilphead and Inverness, and only half a mile away is BT's 'Oban Radio' ship-to-shore HF radio station. The ROC building also has UHF aerials visible which enables it to communicate with military aircraft. If Connel is indeed part of INCA then it is a vital part of the USA's means to command and control a European nuclear war, and would be one of the most important Soviet targets in Scotland in such a war.

Connel may also be, or have been, part of the Washington–Moscow 'hot line', which until 1978 relied on a land and submarine cable carrying telex messages. Although the cable link was replaced by a satellite communications system in January 1978, there is some evidence that the cable system was retained as back-up. Many people consider the 'hot line', which was established in 1963 following the Cuban missile crisis, to be a valuable facility for defusing crises and therefore reducing tension between the superpowers which might lead to war. However, Ball stresses its importance not in preventing, but in conducting a nuclear war, and quotes US Secretary for Defense Schlesinger to this effect: 'If we were to maintain continued communications with the Soviet leaders during the war, and if we were to describe precisely and meticulously the limited nature of our actions, including the desire to avoid attacking their urban industrial base . . . political leaders on both sides will be under powerful pressure to continue to be sensible.'[11] So even the 'hot line' is seen by the US, if not the Soviet, leadership as part of a 'limited' nuclear war-fighting strategy.

The ROC building is on the edge of the wartime Connel airfield, which is occasionally used by Army Air Corps Beaver and RAF Hercules aircraft, probably in connection with army exercises locally, but again, possibly in connection with the ROC communications centre.

30. Daliburgh, South Uist   TAVR small-arms range.

31. Dingwall, Easter Ross   TAVR small-arms range.

32. Dounreay, Caithness   Commonly referred to as a civilian nuclear research plant, though civil and military nuclear interests are notoriously hard to separate.

The Vulcan Naval Nuclear Propulsion Test Establishment (formerly HMS *Vulcan*), Dounreay has been involved in nuclear submarine engine projects since 1957; this was not disclosed until 1960. At that time the 'civil' UKAEA and the main engine contractors, Rolls-Royce and Vickers, were working with the navy on a prototype power plant known as DSMP (Dounreay Submarine Prototype) on a site adjacent to the experimental 'civil' reactor. Problems with leaky pipework and the eventual availability of US propulsion technology led to the navy's first SSN, HMS *Dreadnought,* being powered by a US reactor. Improvements to DSMP followed and derivative reactors powered subsequent British nuclear submarines. Since 1959 Rolls-Royce Associates Ltd has acted as the navy's agent for reactor design and procurement.

A second shore test facility on the same site as DSMP, for the PWR 2 design, was completed in 1982 at a cost of £100 million. This is a test facility for the reactor needed to power the navy's Type 640 Trident SSBNs. The PWR 2 reactor itself was being completed at Barrow in 1983 and due to be shipped to Dounreay on an ocean-going barge in 1984.

Plutonium nitrate from the adjacent UKAEA Prototype Fast Reactor is shipped out to Windscale for reprocessing.

33. Forss and West Murkle, Caithness This pair of US navy radio stations near Thurso, known collectively as NAVCOMM-STAUK (Naval Communications Station UK), was built during a major phase of US expansion in Europe and the Northern Waters, including the deployment of Polaris SSBNs to Holy Loch.

West Murkle was opened in 1963 to provide facilities for relaying command and control messages to US naval units, notably SSBNs, in the north-east Atlantic and the Norwegian Sea. It shared this role with a similar station near Derry in Northern Ireland until the latter closed in 1975–76 and its role was transferred to Forss.

West Murkle has 12 receiving masts and a Defense Satellite Communications System (DSCS) satellite ground terminal under a large green 'golf ball' radome visible from Scrabster Pier. The DSCS, which uses a large number of specialised satellites, is an SHF, high-capacity, long-distance strategic communications system, providing secure, unjammable voice and data links for the US World Wide Military Command and Control System (WWMCCS) and the US armed forces generally. At US discretion,

DSCS is also available to other US agencies, NATO and the British MOD. It also transmits back to the USA 'some surveillance, intelligence and early-warning data collected overseas.'[12]

Forss, opened in 1965, is the transmitter station, with 25 masts dominated by a 610ft high VLF aerial which became operational at the end of 1977. Three log periodic arrays provide directional transmission, probably using LF, to distant receivers. Forss is also one of the US navy's 40–50 fixed HF radio stations used as back-up for its VLF and LF systems. The power radiated from these transmitters accounts for the separation of West Murkle and Forss; induction problems would be caused by placing the transmitters and receivers together. Forss also maintains the UKMS microwave chain up the east coast from Edzell to its northern terminus at West Murkle.

Radio communications

Radio waves can be transmitted over a range of frequency bands from Extremely Low Frequency (ELF), the lowest frequency generally usable, up through VLF, LF, MF, HF, VHF, and UHF to SHF and EHF. The lower the frequency, the longer the wavelength of the signal, and the greater distance it can travel round the Earth or penetrate down below the ocean's surface. Hence UHF and VHF, which can only travel in a straight line, are used by military aircraft and ground troops for short-range communications, while submerged submarines can only be contacted using ELF (which can be used only for very short messages down to about 350 feet below the surface), VLF (down to 50 feet) or LF (near the surface).

The two bases have a total staff of 152, with some 200 dependants and 54 civilian employees. There is also a 12 man RAF detachment here which maintains the satellite communications terminal and the HF receiver.

Both bases have an important function within the WWMCCS, which provides command and control of US nuclear forces, in particular the relay of Emergency Action Messages (EAMS) ordering the use of nuclear weapons. West Murkle/Forss can relay command messages to submarines below or near the sea surface and to the US navy's EC-130Q TACAMO aircraft; one of these is on continuous patrol over both the Atlantic and the Pacific, to relay messages to submerged SSBNs by VLF radio using a 5 mile length of wire trailed by the aircraft. By keeping the aircraft in a continuous tight turn the wire hangs near-vertically and acts as an aerial. The US navy regards TACAMO as 'the only reliable system for communicating the EAM [to SSBNs] in the event of a nuclear exchange.'[13] This would, however, depend on there being undamaged airbases for the EC-130Qs to land and refuel – including those in Scotland.

The HF systems at Forss and West Murkle can be used to communicate with ships and with US ASW or strike aircraft at long range.

The US navy has only six main VLF transmitter sites, none of which is in the UK. Forss is one of the secondary stations, which also include Grindavik in Iceland, and probably Anthorn in Cumbria and the 'NATO' site at Novika in Norway. Use of these facilities at Forss by the RN and other NATO forces is only as a subsidiary to US requirements. A VLF transmitter identical to the one at Forss was erected in Iceland in 1981 and officially described as not being required for 'use by or in support of a US unit committed to NATO.'[14] Other facilities at Thurso are also in firmly non-NATO categories. In fact Forss and West Murkle duplicate many of the naval communications facilities run by the RN at Crimond, thereby ensuring that the USA does not have to rely on its allies for communications.

The importance of these two bases to the USA is reflected in the fact that they were graced by the presence of the highest ranking US navy officer – the Chief of Naval Operations – during Christmas 1980. Since the US navy is not permitted to have permanent bases in Norway, it must provide communications for its forces in the north-east Atlantic and Norwegian Sea from Scotland and Iceland. As the US navy continues its unprecedented expansion to 600 ships, arms nuclear attack submarines and surface ships with thousands of sea-launched cruise missiles, and operates on a more aggressive footing with deployment far forward in the Norwegian and Barents Seas,

Forss and West Murkle will become even more vital in the US attempt to control its sea-based nuclear forces.

US communications networks

The USA retains its own private strategic communications network within the NATO area so that US 'global options' remain unhindered by minor obstacles such as possible disapproval of US actions by 'host' governments. These private systems free the USA from any reliance on the likes of British Telecom.

The US systems present in Scotland are mainly extensions of the Defense Communications System (DCS) which is itself part of the World Wide Military Command and Control System (WWMCCS). The DCS interconnects the three military networks shared between the US forces – the Defense Switched Network (DSN), which provides an automatic non-secure worldwide telephone network; AUTOSEVOCOM (Automatic Secure Voice Communications), which is an encrypted telephone system; and the Defense Data Network (DDN), which provides worldwide digital data links between computers, with some circuits leased to NATO.

All three of these are likely to be present at US bases in Scotland. Transmission methods include cable, microwave, troposcatter, HF and satellite. The USA also uses NATO-owned circuits but ensures that actual control of these rests with the USA and is not pre-emptable by NATO.

In another part of the DCS, the US navy runs the UK Microwave System (UKMS) in Scotland. This is in turn part of the Digital European Backbone (DEB) which links US activities in the UK, Belgium, West Germany and Italy and has been specifically mentioned in relation to the allocation of US-controlled tactical nuclear weapons to NATO for 'Selected Nuclear Release'.[15] The UKMS originally linked Forss, West Murkle, Mormond Hill and Edzell with the US navy communications station near Derry, but since the latter's closure it seems that all parts of the UKMS south-west of Kinnaber are out of use. The installations are nevertheless still in place and could be reactivated for 'contingencies'. The UKMS shares several sites with British Telecom microwave relays used by the MOD, and also interconnects with ACE HIGH, 'enabling exchanges and circuit extensions'.[16] This may suggest US eavesdropping on British military signals, as described by Campbell.[17]

Other US communications systems in Scotland are the North

Atlantic Relay System (NARS), used for relaying BMEWS data from Fylingdales and anti-submarine data from SOSUS, and satellite links which are used for fast relay of bulk intelligence and surveillance data.

---

34. Fort George, Inverness This imposing structure, originally built to suppress the natives during the Jacobite rebellions, has been used in the post-war period as a battalion-strength infantry barracks, complete with small-arms, grenade and mortar ranges which were also used in the 1970s by foreign internal security units such as the Federal German *Bundesgrenschutz*. The last infantry unit left in 1980. More recently Fort George has been a main centre for the government's £1.5 million scheme to encourage young unemployed people to appreciate military life through 'adventure training'. This is an extension of the base's role as the main Joint Services Mountain Training Centre for Scotland.

In June 1983 John Laing Construction began a £13.25 million redevelopment of Fort George. Completion is due in 1985 but by late 1984 an infantry battalion, probably from the Black Watch, will have taken up residence.

35. Glenmore, Aviemore Army outdoor training centre, bought in 1983.

36. Grantown-on-Spey MOD (Air) (i.e. Meteorological Office) automatic weather station, built on a hillside above the town in 1977–78. This station is believed to perform an important role in recording weather data for use by low-flying military aircraft in the Highlands. Grantown also houses an RAF Adventure Training Centre.

37. Gruinard Island, Wester Ross In 1941 this island, which is less than half a mile offshore, was poisoned with anthrax in a series of secret experiments to determine the feasibility of using germ warfare against German cities. These tests were judged to be 'successful' but the germ bombs were not used. A full history of these tests can be read elsewhere.[18]

Access to Gruinard has been forbidden since 1941 to all but specially inoculated and clad scientists from the Microbiological Research Establishment (MRE) at Porton Down. The anthrax spores are still active and in 1972 the cost of decontamination was put at £20 million.[19]

In the late 1970s a party of children and adults on a boat trip suffered an engine failure and drifted on to Gruinard. The MRE assured those involved that they were in no danger from the anthrax. Similar assurances have been given to other unintending visitors, including an Austrian tourist in 1982. A very different reaction occured in 1981 when a group of 'environmentalists' calling themselves 'Dark Harvest' claimed to have removed 300 lb of soil from the island in protest at its continued pollution. Small amounts of soil were left outside Porton Down and up the Blackpool Tower during the Conservative Party Conference, and although these were never proved to have come from Gruinard, a massive investigation was launched to try to find the culprits.

The west coast of Scotland has had a continued relationship with Britain's chemical and biological warfare programme since the war. Between 1945 and 1948 about 100,000 tons of British chemical weapons were dumped in the sea off the Hebrides. A further 8,000 tons were disposed of in the same way in 1956–57. In 1952, without any public consultation, germ warfare agents were released in an experiment off Lewis. Similar releases occurred in 1957 and 1958 off the west coast.

38. Invergordon, Easter Ross RN oil fuel depot and pier, with oil tanks covering 78 acres in the town connected by pipeline to an underground oil storage site at Inchindown, three miles north-west of Invergordon. The facilities were built before the First World War and Invergordon was a major naval port and dockyard until 1956. Since then, use of the oil fuel depot has been primarily by Royal Fleet Auxiliary (RFA) tankers taking on fuel for replenishment of warships at sea during NATO exercises. As the Falklands war showed, these are likely to include vessels carrying nuclear weapons.

The Invergordon pier is also used by the RAF marine craft from Alness. Invergordon was announced as one of the naval shore facilities to close as a result of John Nott's cuts in June 1981. The depot was to be run down from 1984 and closed in 1986 with the loss of 27 civilian jobs, but in March 1983 a review of the MOD's fuel requirements in the light of the Falklands war led to a reassessment of the plans for Invergordon. A decision was due in mid-1983.

39. Inverness TAVR centre – a detachment of 205 (Scottish) General Hospital, RAMC(V), and C Company, 2nd Battalion 51st Highland Volunteers.

40. Inverness (Cameron Barracks) Army infantry depot, training base and REME Support Group, and Regimental HQ of the Queen's Own Highlanders. The base was used as a joint army/RAF Tactical Operations Centre during exercise 'Snowy Owl' in 1972, and there are regular visits by army, RAF and marines helicopters on exercises.

41. Inverness (Longman) MOD (Air) fuel depot, operated by the British Pipeline Agency. Aviation fuel (kerosene) is delivered to Inverness harbour by coastal tanker and fed into storage bunkers on the Longman. An 8 inch diameter pipeline, whose construction angered many farmers along its route, conveys the fuel eastwards to RAF Kinloss and Lossiemouth. In 1983 a new pumping station was installed inside a large hardened bunker to boost the fuel flow and ensure an unhindered supply to the Nimrods and Buccaneers operating out of the two Moray airbases in wartime. This facility makes Inverness a vital supply point for the military and hence a likely Soviet target – as it was assumed to be in exercise 'Square Leg' in 1980.

42. Inverness (Raigmore) HQ 30 Group Royal Observer Corps (ROC), controlling about 40 ROC posts from Pitlochry to Shetland. The ROC took over this bunker from a Royal Auxiliary Air Force fighter control unit in 1962. The HQ's role is to collect, collate and plot nuclear blast and fall-out data relayed from the monitoring posts under its control, and to transmit the results by landline to UKWMO Caledonian Sector Control at Craigiebarns House, Dundee. There are also British Telecom landline/microwave links from Raigmore to other ROC Group Controls at Prestwick and Aberdeen and to the ROC Communications Centre at Connel.

In 1982 the rather ancient teleprinters at Raigmore were replaced by automatic message processing and switching equipment linked to video display units, all of these hardened against nuclear effects such as electro-magnetic pulse to improve the unit's 'survivability' in a nuclear war.

Raigmore has three crews of 43 ROC personnel each. When fully manned the bunker has one and a half crews on duty, with BT engineers and other support personnel bringing the total wartime crewing of the bunker to between 80 and 90. Three 8 hour and one 24 hour exercises are held each year. Group Controls also participate in periodic NATO-wide civil defence exercises.

43. Kingussie TAVR Adventure Training Centre.

44. Kyle of Lochalsh, Wester Ross British Underwater Test and Evaluation Centre (BUTEC). This is the main trials range for torpedoes and other undersea warfare equipment in Britain. It is run by the Ranges and Ships Division of the Admiralty Underwater Weapons Establishment (AUWE) on behalf of the RN's Director of Underwater Weapons Projects, and is primarily responsible for development trials of heavyweight torpedoes and underwater test vehicles, although it was also involved in development of the Stingray lightweight torpedo which entered service on Nimrods and Sea King helicopters during the Falklands war. BUTEC is also used to demonstrate British underwater weapons to foreign customers and for training RAF Nimrod and RN Sea King, ship and submarine crews in torpedo firing. Submarines account for 95 per cent of torpedo firings at BUTEC. Since these rarely surface and most of the instrumentation is underwater, the range area has a deceptively tranquil appearance on the surface.

The main work of BUTEC since 1980 has been development of the new Marconi (MSDS) 7525 Spearfish heavyweight torpedo. This will be the main armament of the RN's expanding SSN fleet for the rest of this century. Between August 1980 and May 1981, MSDS conducted about 45 trial runs of the Spearfish prototypes at BUTEC, testing its controllability, target acquisition, speed (up to 70 knots) and self-generated noise characteristics.

The range area covers about 10 square miles of the Inner Sound of Raasay, off the east coast of Raasay, while the danger area extends to around 130 square miles. There are 15 hydrophone arrays mounted on 2 metre poles on the seabed to monitor and track the torpedoes and test vehicles. Eight Royal Maritime Auxiliary Service (RMAS) boats are used to patrol the range, recover torpedoes and maintain sonar equipment, including active sonars which are lowered into the water to simulate the sounds of ships and submarines and act as targets for homing torpedoes.

BUTEC was first proposed in 1971. Operations began in 1973, with shore facilities limited to an office on the railway pier at Kyle, portacabins at Applecross, 40 MOD personnel and 20 civil employees. By 1981 BUTEC had expanded to include a £3 million shore base and pier at Kyle, a range control building at Applecross, a hostel at Balmacara, a research establishment on Rona, a helicopter base at Broadford, 16 houses in the area, 60 MOD staff and 140 civil employees, with plans in hand to more than double the restricted zone around the range and expand the base at Kyle, despite vociferous local opposition, particularly from fishermen.

There are five main shore facilities associated with BUTEC:

(a) Kyle of Lochalsh: Shore Support Base, built 1977–78 on a 4 acre site earmarked by Highland Regional Council as an industrial estate, with a new pier capable of handling 6,000 ton ships which is the base for the eight RMAS vessels used on the range. The base consists of a main office building, a radio direction-finding building, torpedo and equipment storage areas and a helipad which is also used for fuse balancing of torpedoes.

(b) Rhu-na-Lachan, Applecross: Range Control, established with portacabins in 1973. A permanent building was built in 1978–79. This is linked to the hydrophone complex under the Sound of Raasay by undersea cable. Computer facilities process the sonar data and provide instrumentation for torpedo firings. Command and control of operations on the range is provided by VHF and UHF radio from here.

(c) Broadford, Skye: Highland Regional Council-owned airstrip built by the army in 1972. Since 1979 Bristow Helicopters have used this as a base for their contract work for BUTEC. One helicopter is based here and used primarily for daily flights transporting personnel from Balmacara and Kyle to Rona and Applecross. It is not used for range patrol duties because of its high running costs. A block landing fee of £7,000 per annum is paid to the council. The airstrip is also used for air transport of test torpedoes to and from Marconi's factory near Southampton, and occasionally by RN helicopters engaged on trials work on the range.

(d) Balmacara: Accommodation hostel for 37 RN and some civil contractors' personnel, leased from the regional council for 30 years from 1980. Personnel are flown to and from the BUTEC range sites each day by helicopter.

(e) Rona: Admiralty Marine Technology Establishment (AMTE) sonar research and range facility. Work carried out here includes the analysis and classification of the underwater sound characteristics ('sonar signatures') of different types of ship and submarine. This is used to build up a library of sound characteristics which can be fed into sonar system computers on board ASW vessels and aircraft, and used to identify targets as well as process out the noise made by friendly vessels. Rona has no direct operational function but its work is vital to the RN's ASW capability.

The Admiralty has had a sonar research and development facility on Rona since the 1950s. This was greatly expanded when BUTEC was established. Rona's facilities now include a main operational building, a house for the resident RN officer and pier facilities in Loch a'Bhraige. The installation controls the 'AMTE Rona Ranger', a sonar range in the northern part of the Sound of Raasay, separate from the BUTEC torpedo range. Regular trials are conducted with submerged nuclear and diesel submarines. The establishment is run by about 37 civilian engineers and technicians employed by MSDS and RCA, the two main BUTEC contractors. They are flown in daily from Kyle and Balmacara by helicopter.

Rona was expanded in 1977 with virtually no consultation with any civil authority. The Highland Regional Council Planning Department was informed of the MOD's intention to develop Rona by letter on 9 February 1977. Faced with the MOD *fait accompli* that construction was due to start at the end of that month, the council merely sent a rubber-stamp letter of approval six days later. Within two weeks, local people were amazed to see ships and helicopters ferrying building materials to the remote island, at enormous cost. The new installation cost £1 million to build and was operational in 1978. A photograph of it appeared in the AMTE's recruitment brochure in 1980.[20]

Operation and maintenance of the BUTEC range is carried out by RCA Service Division Ltd, of Middlesex, who provide hardware and software engineers, mechanical, electrical and electronic technicians, small boat crews, and domestic and clerical staff at a cost of about £500,000 a year. Patrolling the range area to prevent repetitions of the damage to hydrophones by fishing boats in 1976, 1977 and 1980 costs at least a further £500,000.

45. Latheron, Caithness Microwave relay station, part of the US navy UKMS, linking Mormond Hill to West Murkle.

46. Ledaig, Barra Racal-Decca Hi-Fix/6 transmitter station built in 1982 for the RN. Hi-Fix is a medium-frequency radio positioning system which can give a ship's position to an accuracy of a few metres up to a range of 300 kilometres. Ledaig is one of a new chain of these unmanned, remote-controlled beacons 'to aid mine detection covering strategic areas of British coastal waters.'[21] Racal-Decca was awarded a £5 million contract for this chain in 1981. Its aim is to keep the SSBN and SSN exit routes from the Clyde open in wartime.

47. Loch Linnhe, Argyll Three NATO mooring buoys were installed here, west of Ballachulish Ferry, in 1962. They are thought to be connected to the UK's Defence Communications Network via the British Telecom trunk cable which runs nearby. The buoys would be used as a wartime emergency anchorage for NATO vessels. There is no record of any peacetime use but they may be earmarked as one of the dispersal sites for the US navy SSBN mother ship from Holy Loch, which can perform its role of rearming and maintaining Poseidon SSBNs independent of shore facilities.

48. Mangersta, Lewis Unmanned NATS radio relay station. Provides voice radio coverage to civil and military aircraft west of the Hebrides on VHF and UHF. Messages are relayed automatically to and from SCATCC at Prestwick by microwave and landline.

49. Meikle Tarrel, Easter Ross This small building overlooking the approaches to Tain bombing range is described in the Valuation Roll as 'Admiralty premises'. It is believed to perform an observation or monitoring function, possibly associated with the bombing range. In this case the reference to it being an Admiralty establishment is probably an out-of-date listing from 1972 or earlier when Tain range was operated by the Fleet Air Arm.

50. Mellon Charles, Wester Ross RN Boom Defence Depot, maintaining anti-submarine defences, which ceased operations in September 1977 and closed in March 1978 with the loss of 14 civilian jobs. Mellon Charles is the last remnant of the wartime Loch Ewe naval anchorage and is now kept on a care and maintenance basis for reactivation in emergency, with 13 employees.

51. Rothiemurchus Lodge, Aviemore Army Adventure Training Centre.

52. St Kilda Missile tracking and sea-watch radar station for Royal Artillery Range, Hebrides. St Kilda's civilian population was evacuated at its own request in 1930, and the St Kilda group subsequently became National Trust for Scotland property, leased to the Nature Conservancy as a nature reserve. The military invasion began in 1957 when an RAF construction team arrived for the original 'Operation Hard Rock'. A large chunk of the hillside in Village Bay, Hirta, was blasted out to provide construction material and by 1959 an army radar station was established on Mullach Mor, the second highest point on Hirta, to provide surveillance of ships and aircraft entering the range danger area. Although only two men are required to operate the radar during missile firing, over 30 troops are stationed on Hirta, mostly on six-week detachments from Benbecula, to provide technical and domestic support. In 1974 £1 million was spent on building a new centrally-heated mess with full kitchen facilities, a bar and medical quarters, in marked contrast to the poverty and extremely hard conditions which forced the St Kildans to emigrate in 1930. The troops on St Kilda are supplied in summer by one of the army's two Landing Craft

Logistics (LCLs) which ships food, fuel and equipment from Rhu and Carnan Jetty to St Kilda about once a fortnight. In winter supply drops are made by chartered civil helicopter (usually from Aberdeen) at a cost of several thousand pounds a time.

In the early days of the missile range (1959–66) Corporal and Sergeant tactical nuclear missiles were being fired; their 20–75 mile range gave the St Kilda detachment some role in instrumentation of missile firings. Since 1968 most missile firings have been short-range Rapier and Blowpipe surface-to-air missiles, so St Kilda's role has been restricted mainly to radar surveillance of the range danger area. In 1976, however, the first British army firing of the Lance tactical nuclear missile took place from South Uist, and from 1977 about 15 Lance firings a year have been carried out, giving St Kilda an increased role again. In 1979 a new Marconi radar was installed on Mullach Mor to cover Lance firings. In 1981 a 250ft radio mast was erected on top of Mullach Mor, part of a new system for destruction of missiles which go out of control. At Mullach Sgar disused radar buildings have been renovated and a new 80ft radio mast and radar installation erected. It is probable that St Kilda already performs a subsidiary air defence role by feeding some of its radar data to the RAF radar station at Benbecula via microwave links to Range Control on Rueval. When the new UKADGE radar station on North Uist is operational in the mid-1980s, St Kilda is likely to have direct links to it for transmission of radar data. It may also become a designated dispersal site for the s-band radar on South Clettraval (it could be transported in five Chinook helicopter loads), since St Kilda would not only provide better range to the north and west because of its position but would have even greater range and low-level coverage because Mullach Mor is 750 feet higher than South Clettraval. St Kilda may also become the location of one of the electronic replica radars which are to be built as decoy targets near UKADGE radar sites. Some hint of an operational role of this sort for St Kilda was given in November 1982 when an RAF Chinook helicopter was seen transporting a Rapier missile unit to St Kilda. This exercise was repeated in February 1983.

53. Sandwick, Lewis NATS (National Air Traffic Services) long-range secondary surveillance radar station. Built in 1973 as the first NATS radar station with secondary radar equipment only (i.e. it only deals with aircraft equipped with IFF transponders), Sandwick provides coverage of the many civil and military aircraft operating at high level (over 25,000 feet) off north-west Scotland, as far west as the limits of British airspace at 10° west. The radar data is transmitted direct to the Scottish Air Traffic Control Centre (SCATCC) at Prestwick where it is processed, with similar data from six other radars in Scotland, and displayed to controllers. Most of the civil aircraft tracked by Sandwick are airliners on transatlantic flights, but NATS is run jointly with the MOD and Sandwick also tracks and controls myriad military aircraft in the area, including a large number of US military transport flights to and from Europe. This would be one of the most important radar stations in Britain for controlling the US air reinforcement of a European war.

Sandwick is also a NATS multi-carrier radio relay station, relaying voice radio messages from SCATCC to civil aircraft (on VHF) and military aircraft (on UHF).

54. Shillay, Monach Islands In 1978 it was announced that the MOD planned to establish an infra-red monitor station on top of the disused lighthouse on Shillay, for basic research by the Royal Aircraft Establishment (RAE) into light transmission through the atmosphere, using heat and light sources, mirrors and lenses. The research would be 'of relevance to low-level air operations at night and submarine warfare'. Shillay was chosen due to the lack of atmospheric pollution and for 'other reasons'.[22] The research was said to be unconnected with the Uist missile range although the Monachs lie within the range danger area, and the Meteorological Office, Science Research Council and Atomic Weapons Research Establishment also conduct atmospheric research from South Uist. It also seems more than coincidental that an infra-red monitor station should be established next to the main firing range for Rapier at a time when an infra-red target detector was being developed for this missile.

The connection with 'low-level air operations at night' is

almost certainly part of the RAE's £4 million 'Nightbird' programme, designed to give the RAF the ability to carry out
single-seat low-level strike/attack missions at night and in poor
weather. One of the RAE's Buccaneers, already a familiar sight
over the West Highlands on trials flights from West Freugh, is
being fitted out with a variety of radar, laser range-finder,
head-up display and forward-looking infra-red (FLIR) equipment and will start trials flights in late 1983. The target
acquisition FLIR, manufactured by Marconi, is steered by a
Ferranti mirror system, which was probably developed from the
Shillay trials. This is another example of the Highlands and
Islands being used to develop NATO's offensive capability. The
RAE's work at Shillay and elsewhere has allowed its Hunter
research aircraft 'to be flown at night through twisting Welsh
valleys at speeds of up to 530 knots and heights down to 200
feet',[23] and will undoubtedly lead to similar very low and fast
flying at night in Scotland in the near future.

The reference to submarine warfare suggests that the research at Shillay is connected with the development of infra-red
sensors which can detect a submerged submarine's wake as it
reaches the surface. This will be a further contribution to
NATO's overwhelming superiority in anti-submarine warfare.

55. South Clettraval, North Uist Missile tracking radar for
Royal Artillery Range, Hebrides, linked to Rueval (Range
Control) by microwave radio. In 1981 construction work started
on a new radar station here, part of the UKADGE update (for
details, see Benbecula and pp. 18–21); completion is due in
1983 but the station is not expected to be operational until
1985–86.

56. South Uist Royal Artillery Range, Hebrides; various
sites, listed below from north to south:

(a) Carnan Jetty: Royal Corps of Transport port facility,
used by LCLS taking supplies to and from Rhu and St Kilda.

(b) West Geirinish: Rangehead; technical headquarters of
range, with four missile launch areas (two for Rapier, two for
Lance) and a launch area for ASAT target drones.

(c) Rueval: Range Control; command and control of the
range area, including missile tracking and instrumentation and

communication between range sites.

(d) Rubha Ardvule: Launch area for Skeet target aircraft and Blowpipe missiles.

(e) Sheaval: Unmanned sea-watch radar covering southern part of range area.

(f) Lochboisdale: Moorings for the three range patrol boats and a 115 ft trawler used from summer 1982 as a target ship.

The Royal Artillery Guided Weapons Range, Hebrides, provides operational training for units operating Rapier and Blowpipe anti-aircraft missiles and Lance surface-to-surface tactical nuclear missiles. Subsidiary functions include firing of upper atmosphere research rockets; trials flying of reconnaissance drones (small pilotless aircraft) such as the CT-89; trials firing of air-to-air missiles (e.g. RAF AIM-7E2 Sparrows in 1978); and use of the range for simulated attacks by RAF aircraft.

The British Aerospace Dynamics Group Rapier is a short-range surface-to-air missile in service with six squadrons of the RAF Regiment (four in Germany, one each at Lossiemouth and Leuchars) and three Light Air Defence Regiments of the Royal Artillery (the 12th and 22nd in Germany plus one in the UK) Each of these nine units spends a two-week period at South Uist every year on missile practice camp, firing anything up to 40 missiles a day from the two launch areas on the sand dunes at West Geirinish. In 1981 the MOD ordered the Tracked Rapier (a missile fire unit mounted on a modified armoured personnel carrier), to equip three mobile air defence batteries in BAOR from 1983 at a cost of over £235 million. Tracked Rapier was tested at South Uist in 1979–80 and when in operational service will conduct practice firings there. In 1980, as part of the UK–US deal to offset the cost of Britain buying Trident missiles, the USAF bought $500 million-worth of Rapiers, to be operated by three new RAF Regiment squadrons which will defend USAF air bases in the UK against air attack. These will also be training at South Uist from late 1983, so a major increase in Rapier firings there is in prospect. Rapiers are fired at Rushton targets towed on a 4 mile long cable by RAF Canberra TT.18s which operate from Kinloss. This is an enormously expensive exercise; each day's firing involves about 10 hours of Canberra flying at about £7,000 an hour, and each Rapier missile costs £9,000. Most of the missiles miss the target; the miss distance is measured by a radioactivity monitor in the target which calculates the amount of radiation given off by a ¾ inch by ½ inch isotope mounted in each missile. The isotopes are transported to South Uist, 120 at at time, about every two months, on civilian lorries aboard the Cal-Mac ferry to Lochmaddy. This was only revealed when one of the lorries went into a ditch on North Uist in June 1979. No comment has been made about the thousands of isotopes now lying on the seabed amongst the wreckage of missiles, and their effects on marine life and fishing in the area.

To reduce the vulnerability of Rapier firings to bad weather and reduce the costs of operating the range, targets towed by Canberras are to be phased out by 1984 and replaced by the high-speed, highly manoeuvrable Advanced Subsonic Aerial Target (ASAT) target drone, launched from a 115 metre diameter 'racetrack' which was under construction at West Geirinish in 1982. When ASAT is in use the Rapiers will no longer be firing merely at a target flying straight and level at relatively slow speed; ASAT can perform 6g turns and fly at up to 450 knots – simulating the performance of an attacking aircraft. This increases the chances of a missile going off course or out of control. The missiles can be destroyed in flight, and most of those that do go out of control crash into the sea, but there is no guarantee that a destroyed missile's debris will not fall on populated or agricultural land.

The Shorts Blowpipe is a light, short-range surface-to-air missile fired from the shoulder. It is in service with two army regiments in Germany, three TAVR Air Defence regiments in Britain, and the Royal Marines (also in Argentina, Canadian forces in Germany, and others). Another 12 TAVR detachments are currently being equipped with Blowpipe in a £20 million order announced in 1980. Each Blowpipe operator carries out one live missile firing a year, with new trainees firing two in their first year. Some of this firing takes place at Otterburn and Larkhill ranges in England but about 500 firings a year are carried out on South Uist, from a launch site at Rubha Ardvule,

10 miles south of the rangehead. Blowpipe is fired at model aircraft targets – currently the Shorts Skeet and MATS-B – which are also launched from Rubha Ardvule. In 1982 a programme of improvements to Blowpipe, including a 400 per cent increase in warhead lethality and a semi-automatic guidance system, was under way at a cost of more than £200 million, and with more TAVR units expected to be equipped with Blowpipe, the number of practice firings at South Uist is likely to increase.

The Vought MGM-52C Lance is a tactical nuclear missile with a·W-70 warhead of 10 kilotons (only slightly less than the Hiroshima bomb) and a maximum range of 75 miles. The BAOR's 50th Missile Regiment has 12 Lance launchers which would be used against concentrations of Warsaw Pact armoured and other forces in the German border area. The Lance was first fired at South Uist in 1976 and operational firings began in 1977. The 50th Missile Regiment spends one or two fortnights at South Uist each year, firing about 15 missiles. The nuclear warheads are left behind in Germany; Lances fired from South Uist have concrete dummy warheads. The 'targets' are co-ordinates in the sea, in international waters south of St Kilda. Also at South Uist are personnel from the Meteorological Office Rockets Division and the Atomic Weapons Research Establishment, the latter under the guise of the innocent-sounding Science Research Council. They are engaged in firing atmospheric research rockets and other research activity. Much of the early research carried out by these rocket firings in the 1960s was connected with nuclear missile targeting and nuclear explosion characteristics and it is likely that this is still one of their prime functions. AWRE had eight caravans for personnel at West Geirinish in 1975–76; development of the new warheads for Trident will almost certainly include further AWRE research work at South Uist.

The South Uist site was identified in 1955 as the location for a major guided weapons range, including an 8,000 ft runway for pilotless aircraft at Sollas in North Uist. In 1957 this was scaled down to an army range only, for tactical nuclear missiles – Corporal and Sergeant – operating in spring and summer only. With such limited use, the range was under threat of closure in the mid-1960s but in 1968 a major expansion was announced, taking over 1,350 acres of machair land to make way for anti-aircraft missile firing as well as the new Lance.

The military in the Uists have given at least two assurances since 1967 that there would be no further expansion; these promises have been consistently broken, and further fears were raised in 1982 when news emerged (not from the MOD) that US army officers had inspected the range as a possible replacement for the NATO Missile Firing Installation in Crete.

Safety aspects of missile firing at South Uist are kept quiet by the MOD, but it is not unusual for missiles to go out of control. Most of these are destroyed in mid-air before they can cause damage, but in May 1966 a Corporal missile turned east after launch, screamed over houses in South Uist (narrowly missing a manse and a hamlet) and crashed in Loch Druidibeg, miraculously without any casualties. Stories abound of mysterious explosions on hillsides in Wester Ross; these may have a South Uist connection.

57. Stornoway, Lewis MOD-owned airfield, currently being upgraded for the second time in 20 years as a NATO Forward Operating Base (FOB) at an official cost of £40 million. The current construction programme dates from 1973, when ownership of the airfield was suddenly transferred from the Civil Aviation Authority (CAA) to the MOD; the CAA continues to operate the airfield as a civil airport.

Stornoway's expansion involves a 1,600 ft runway extension, nine hardened aircraft shelters, bulk fuel installations, new radar and navigation aids, a new control tower and operations buildings, married quarters and barracks. It is said by the MOD to be for use as an air defence FOB for RAF Phantoms initially, being replaced by Tornados in the late 1980s. However, Stornoway has been an FOB for NATO maritime patrol aircraft since 1964 and for maritime strike Buccaneers in the early to mid-1970s. The airfield has been used regularly by target-towing Canberras and anti-submarine Sea King helicopters during exercises, and by a variety of RAF aircraft as a practice diversion airfield (reflecting the inclusion of the Western Isles in the areas permitted for low-flying since 1979). Until March 1982 the airfield was also the base of 112 Signals Unit, RAF, whose function was to monitor simulated bombing runs and electronic counter-measures transmissions of RAF Vulcans and other offensive aircraft training for nuclear strike missions. Most of 112 SU's personnel were dispersed in March 1982 but a small body of RAF staff is retained to maintain RAF navigation and radio equipment on the airfield and to operate the radio station at Aird Uig.

The key function of an expanded NATO base at Stornoway will be to support US air and sea reinforcement of Europe both by providing forward air defence of the transatlantic sea lanes and as a refuelling stop for US combat and transport aircraft. The planned construction of hardened aircraft shelters confirms NATO's intention to use Stornoway as part of a war-fighting strategy.

NATO expansion plans at Stornoway have been consistently opposed by Western Isles Council since 1978 and by the broad-based campaigning group Keep NATO Out (KNO) since 1979, reflecting widespread local objections to the proposals. This opposition forced the authorities to hold a public inquiry in 1981, but democracy was suspended in the interests of militarism and the development was approved despite the acknowledged success of the opposition case. In late 1982 the first phase of the redevelopment, the £8 million runway extension, was put out to tender, for construction from spring 1983. The rules of the NATO Infrastructure Programme funding are that tenders must go out to all NATO countries, but in this case tender documents went only to seven British companies. This suggests that NIP funds have not been forthcoming and the development is proceeding on a piecemeal basis with funds from the British defence budget.

Even a cancellation of the existing expansion programme would not rule out increased military use of Stornoway. Many aircraft, including C-5s and C-141s operating in wartime conditions, are capable of landing and taking off on the existing runway. Stornoway has supported exercises involving up to 50 military aircraft movements a day, and the Western Isles are increasingly used for low-flying. Construction of the new UKADGE radar station in the Uists will also bring more aircraft to Stornoway during air defence exercises.

In April 1983 Costain's started work on the £8 million first phase – lengthening the runway at both ends, building a new taxiway, widening the perimeter track and constructing aircraft hardstandings. Completion is due in October 1984. As predicted by KNO, the 'jobs boom' is an illusion; Costain's are employing only 30–40 local people.

Further confirmation of KNO's predictions about future use of an expanded airbase at Stornoway came in February 1983 with an article in the US magazine *Aviation Week and Space Technology*. This revealed that the Pentagon's Defense Nuclear Agency, responsible for research and development into the effects of nuclear weapons and optimisation of tactics for their use, had been conducting a feasibility study since 1981 which could lead to deployment of the anti-ship version of the Tomahawk cruise missile around choke-points such as the Greenland–Iceland–UK gap, with the aim of bottling up the Soviet fleet.[24]

The British MOD denied all knowledge of the study, confirming once again the Pentagon's lack of interest in consultation when seeking bases overseas. The results of the study were due in June 1983.

The idea of ground-launched anti-ship Tomahawks deployed around choke-points was in fact raised as early as 1980, apparently by the manufacturers in an attempt to sell more missiles by finding new roles for cruise. The idea was then taken up by a prominent naval analyst in the Brookings Institution, Michael MccGwire, and aired in an authoritative book on cruise missiles in 1981. MccGwire's analysis included consideration of nuclear warheads for these missiles. He stated that

domestic sensitivity to such deployments in the Norwegian Sea area might have to be overcome, but this is likely to diminish as the Soviet surface build-up becomes increasingly obtrusive. Nor is it essential that land-based TASMS [Tomahawk Anti-Ship Missiles] be pre-positioned. For example, missiles could be flown into Iceland during a crisis build-up, joined with simple trailer-launchers stockpiled at Keflavik airbase, and deployed by road to pre-surveyed coastal sites.[25]

KNO had consistently argued that the NATO expansion at Stornoway is not required for the purposes stated by the MOD but is for use by USAF transport and combat aircraft reinforcing US forces in Europe. With the new runway and improved facilities Stornoway would be an attractive location for the military to base a flight of anti-ship cruise missiles, or rapidly deploy them in a crisis.

MccGwire's ideas for cruise deployment in Scotland do not stop at anti-ship missiles. In the same book he argues that nuclear ground-launched cruise missiles have a role to play in support of ground forces on NATO's flanks: 'For example, northern Norway could be covered by ground-launched cruise missiles (GLCMS) emplaced in Scotland'.[26] These plans became a new focus for KNO's campaigning in 1983.

Stornoway airport is also the location of one of the most important meteorological offices in Scotland, one of only three with radiosonde facilities for upper atmosphere measurements. The Met. Office is run by MOD (Air) and is a vital part of the military infrastructure. Upper atmosphere soundings are used, amongst other things, for ballistic missile targeting and fall-out monitoring.

58. Stornoway, Lewis TAVR infantry, one platoon of C Company, 2nd Battalion 51st Highland Volunteers.

59. Tain, Easter Ross RAF bombing range, originally established in 1938, covering 2,486 acres around the disused RAF Tain airfield. Operated by the Fleet Air Arm until 1972, then transferred to the RAF. Tain is one of the most heavily used aerial weapons ranges in the UK, mainly because of its close proximity to Lossiemouth airfield and vast low-flying areas. About 70 per cent of the practice attacks on Tain are made by 226 OCU Jaguars from Lossiemouth, the rest being mostly RAF Jaguars, Buccaneers and Tornados from operational squadrons in the UK and Germany, and USAF F-111s. Since 1981 regular night attacks have been made by RAF Tornados and USAF F-111s flying in the Highlands Restricted Area (see chapter 3), increasing the night use of the range from one day a week to four.

Tain range can handle all manner of low-level attacks with 4 lb and 28 lb practice bombs, cannon and rockets. At maximum capacity Tain may have four aircraft in the circuit pattern over Dornoch and the Dornoch Firth, with attacks being made as often as one every minute. In addition aircraft on low-level strike training flights in the area frequently call up Tain range at the last minute for single passes over the range. At night attacks are made using Lepus flares, dropped four at a time, which flood the entire area with light. The parachutes from these flares have on several occasions fouled the propellors of mussel boats fishing in the Dornoch Firth.

Local people, particularly in Inver and Dornoch, have for many years complained about the disturbance from the range; in 1979–80 the Environmental Health Department of Ross and Cromarty District Council carried out noise measurements and observations of low-flying aircraft and have pressed the MOD to provide soundproofing for local residences and to raise the height limits for aircraft using the range. The MOD responded by saying soundproofing could only be provided around new military installations, and in late 1981 announced that they were seeking to apply the 1938 bye-laws preventing access to the range area more strictly.

RAF Tain has 19 RAF personnel and 7 civilian employees.

60. Tiree A CAA-owned airfield. Two of the three NATS telecommunications maintenance staff here are solely responsible for maintenance of MOD radio equipment. This includes a UHF radio relay on Beinn Hough and an MOD Auto-Triangulation Service receiver on the airfield (installed in 1962). Beinn Hough was until the late 1950s an RAF radar station in the 'Rotor' system and also had a USAF radio navigation beacon until 1958. An empty MOD hut on Beinn Hough is kept on a care and maintenance basis and may be earmarked for rapid installation of military radar or radio equipment. RAF Vulcans have made regular approaches at Tiree and in 1981 a USAF Hercules made a number of landings at the airfield 'to practise diversions to an unfamiliar strip'. Tiree has a 5,800ft runway and may well figure in the military's transatlantic reinforcement or forward operating base plans.

Confirmation of Tiree's potential for supporting US military reinforcement of a European war came early in 1983 when it was announced by the joint civil/military National Air Traffic Services (NATS) that a new 210 nautical mile range radar station, for air traffic control in the Atlantic approaches, was to be built on Ben Hynish at a cost of £8 million. Construction was due to start in spring 1983, and be completed in 1986. All recently installed NATS radars have been made compatible with the UK Air Defence Ground Environment (UKADGE), and Ben Hynish is unlikely to be an exception. This will make Tiree yet another link in the chain of c^3i installations established to support war in Europe.

61. Tulloch, Lochaber Army Mountain Training Centre.

62. Wick, Caithness TAVR infantry, B Company, 3rd Battalion 51st Highland Volunteers.

63. Wick Airport, Caithness A CAA-owned airfield with military facilities, including full NATO-standard approach lighting, an MOD Auto-Triangulation Service UHF D/F receiver (which locates the radio transmissions of military aircraft in distress and transmits the message to the RAF Distress and Diversion Cell at SCATCC Prestwick) and MOD UHF ground-to-air radio facilities. Two of the three NATS telecommunications maintenance staff at Wick are solely responsible for looking after this military equipment. Wick was widely used by the RAF in the 1950s; Leuchars-based Phantoms regularly carried out practice diversions here, and there are weekly visits by the US navy's C-12B communications aircraft from Mildenhall in connection with the two US navy radio stations near Thurso. A large disused weapons store on the north side of the airfield could be readily reactivated and Wick would be a likely wartime forward operating base for air defence aircraft and a stop-over point for transatlantic reinforcements.

Section three: the North-east

64. Aberdeen TAVR units in the city are 51 (Highland) Signal Squadron (v); D (Gordons) Company, 3rd Battalion 51st Highland Volunteers; B Company, 15th (Scottish Volunteer) Battalion, The Parachute Regiment; 252 (Highland) Field Ambulance, RAMC (v); and University Air Squadron, Officers' Training Corps and Naval Units.

65. Aberdeen (Prince of Wales Barracks) Contract Repair Branch, REME, responsible for repairing army vehicles and equipment in the area.

66. Aberdeen (Quarry Road) HQ of 29 Group ROC, controlling about 30 ROC posts in the area, and linked by landline to Raigmore and the Sector Control at Craigiebarns, Dundee. Like the other four ROC Group Controls in Scotland, Quarry Road's prime function is to collect and collate nuclear blast and fall-out data to allow the military to move to 'safe' areas in order to continue fighting a nuclear war.

67. Almondbank, Perth A Royal Navy aircraft workshop. This is one of the three main helicopter repair bases in the UK and is the largest engineering facility in the former county of Perth, employing 450 people.

It houses the Tri-Service Helicopter Component Repair Centre and produces tools as well as components and modification sets for UK military helicopters. A newspaper photograph during the Falklands war showed work in progress on a Nimrod fuselage pannier, possibly to do with modifications for carrying the Harpoon missile.[27] It is not known whether Almondbank performs such work on a regular basis.

Since 1962 Almondbank has been an arms and supply depot for the Federal German navy. When announced, the depot was to have 20–30 German staff under RN control. The site was still in German use in 1974, but a similar site in Cumbria was abandoned in 1977 and Almondbank may have been vacated at this time too.

68. Arbroath, Angus TAVR centre. Base of 212 (Highland) Light Air Defence Battery, Royal Artillery (v), part of 102 (Ulster and Scottish) Air Defence Regiment, armed with

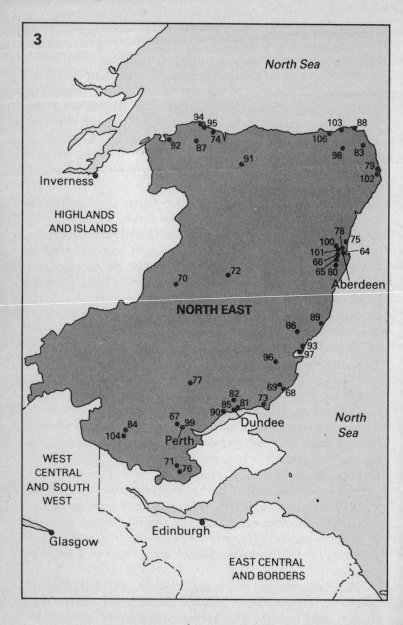

Blowpipe anti-aircraft missiles and assigned in wartime to air defence of military 'vital points' in the British Army of the Rhine's rear areas.

69. Arbroath, Angus Royal Marines camp and airfield, known as 'Condor'. Base of 45 Royal Marine Commando Group, totalling around 1,000 personnel. The 45 Commando is the only marines unit to have fully integrated support units. It consists of three companies of marines; 7 (Sphynx) Battery, 29 Commando Light Regiment Royal Artillery, with 105mm howitzers; a troop of engineers from 59 Independent Commando Squadron, Royal Engineers; a flight of three Gazelle helicopters from 3 Commando Brigade Air Squadron; the Special Boat Squadron (SBS)-trained Commachio Company, and a base support organisation. The 45 Commando is also joined by 140 Dutch marines from W Company, Royal Netherlands Marine Corps, for much of the year.

The 45 Commando moved to Arbroath in 1971 and is fully trained in arctic and mountain warfare. Its role is reinforcement of north Norway, where it spends at least three months each winter in training, culminating in a major amphibious exercise there every March. Since 1978 the Royal Marines have stored 60 Volvo BV202 over-snow vehicles and other equipment in Norway. When not in Norway, 45 Commando trains regularly in the Scottish Highlands and at Barry Buddon.

Commachio Company was formed in May 1980 with a core of SBS men. It is an independent reaction force tasked to deal with security threats to offshore oil and gas installations and to guard the nuclear submarine installations at Faslane, Coulport, Rosyth, and, it is believed, Devonport and Portland. Security of offshore oil installations involves close collaboration between oil companies, the Special Branch, MI5 and Commachio Company. It is a measure of the scale of this unit's little-publicised activities that, at 300 men, it is the largest company in the marines, yet within a year of formation it was seeking authority to recruit a further 96 since 300 was deemed insufficient for the task. The large SBS element in the company wear black waterproof uniforms and are all qualified parachutists, frogmen, divers, small-boat sailors and climbers. They would be transported to oil rigs by RN Sea King helicopters from Prestwick or by RAF Hercules. In 1982 the company conducted a number of exercises involving parachuting into the sea from Hercules transports off Coulport, Lochranza and St Andrews.

In 1980 there were press rumours of the unit moving further north – almost certainly Shetland – but although Commachio conducted one of their 'Prawn Salad/Lobster Pot' oil rig security exercises from a base near Scatsta in April 1983 there is no sign of a permanent move. In fact, although Commachio's main base is Arbroath, its commanding officer is based at HQ Commando Forces in Plymouth, and there is evidence that the unit not only performs base security and anti-terrorist roles at various RN bases but is also engaged, like its US Marine Corps counterparts, in guard and escort duties on nuclear storage sites and convoys.

70. Auchallater, Braemar RAF Expedition Training Area, with almost 14,000 acres used periodically under a licence agreement with the land-owner.

71. Balado Bridge, Kinross NATO communications station, on a former naval airfield which later became an RAF radio station. The latter's MF/HF 'pylon' aerials have largely been dismantled to make way for a satellite ground terminal (SGT) housed in a prominent white 'golf ball' radome beside the public road.

In 1978 Ford Aerospace was awarded an $80 million NATO contract for completion in 1983 of the NATO Satcom Phase III project. This major expansion of fixed and mobile SGTs is part of the NATO Integrated Communications System (NICS) Phase I. SGTs are located 'near the . . . military nerve centres of member nations'[28] since satellite communication is an 'ideal instrument for quick intelligence information and effective command and control.'[29] NATO Satcom Phase III greatly expands maritime satellite links in the NATO area, providing long-distance secure fleet broadcast and two-way links, for example to NATO's Strike Fleet Atlantic.

Balado is part of this expansion. When operational (due in 1983) it is expected to fulfil the satellite communication needs of Pitreavie, to which it will be linked via the MOD's BOXER microwave system. Balado's new satellite terminal underlines

NATO's superiority in the North Atlantic area. NATO has had full satellite communications coverage since 1972 plus access to the US DSCS and UK Skynet satellites. As a rapid data link between Pitreavie and NATO vessels, Balado would have a vital role in command and control of a war in Northern Waters, and be a likely 'time-urgent' target for the USSR.

72. Ballater (Victoria Barracks) This small infantry depot provides grouse-beaters as well as security men for the sporting monarchy at nearby Balmoral.

73. Barry Buddon, Angus Army training camp and ranges covering 2,487 acres of land and 862 acres of foreshore. This was stated in evidence to the Defence Lands Committee in 1972 to be the most important army training area in Scotland.[30] Amongst the uses of the range are firing of all infantry weapons except the heavy anti-tank gun, amphibious training, parachuting and helicopter training. Barry Buddon has also been used by the Ulster Defence Regiment for anti-IRA training.

Although the 1975 Defence Review announced that Barry Buddon would close in 1976, the MOD has retained the site and expanded it despite pressure from various bodies for the release of military land for commercial or recreational development. Nugent noted that 500 acres of the site would be useful for oil-related development in this area of very high unemployment. It was also considered as a site for the Shell–Esso gas fractionation plant instead of Mossmorran, Fife, and in 1981 Tayside Regional Council suggested Barry Buddon as a possible location for Nissan's proposed new car factory, but the MOD were deaf to pleas for the release of land.

Barry Buddon is also of conservation interest, being a Site of Special Scientific Interest (SSSI). The Tayside Study of 1970 identified Barry Links as suitable for intensive recreational development, and suggested a 400 acre country park. The chances of any of these socially useful developments occurring is, however, slim. Following the MOD's abandonment of plans to acquire the Knoydart estate for marines training, Barry Buddon is being expanded. Construction of new accommodation for up to 500 troops commenced in 1983.

74. Binn Hill, Moray TAVR small-arms firing range and training area, covering 74 acres. Also used by RAUXAF Regiment troops from Lossiemouth.

75. Black Dog, Aberdeen Coastal small-arms range used chiefly by infantry trainees from nearby Bridge of Don Barracks.

76. Blair Adam, Kinross TAVR small-arms firing range.

77. Blairgowrie, Perthshire Suggested in 1980 as a probable location for a fallback underground HQ for the Caledonian Sector of the UK Warning and Monitoring Organisation.[31] No evidence of construction has been forthcoming.

78. Bridge of Don (Gordon Barracks), Aberdeen Scottish infantry depot, housing two infantry training battalions. The barracks were extended in 1981–82.

79. Buchan, Peterhead UKADGE/NADGE radar station operated by the RAF. A sign outside station HQ states: 'The job of this station in peace is to prepare for war and don't you forget it.'

This installation is prominently located on a hilltop overlooking Boddam. In the original 'ROTOR' radar system, Buchan was a fully-hardened two-level underground site by 1954. In the subsequent 'Linesman' system Buchan became the 'parent' of the radar stations at Saxa Vord and Benbecula. Under the current upgrading of UKADGE this situation will broadly continue but Saxa Vord and Benbecula will become more autonomous.

Although official statements about the upgrading of UKADGE radar stations have been confusing, Buchan is thought to have no fewer than three radars – a rather dated Plessey Type 80, which can track targets up to 60,000 feet and 200 miles, an HF200 height-finder, and more recently a mobile GE592 D-band surveillance radar. The latter two are housed under green 'golf ball' radomes, the GE592 being trailer-mounted.

A fourth radar will be installed at Buchan in the mid-1980s. This is a Plessey AR320, whose operating frequency enables direct compatibility with the airborne radars on the Nimrod AEW.3 and E-3 AWACS. Both the GE592 and the AR320 can be moved around on five large trailers. In wartime one or both would be moved to pre-surveyed dispersal sites in the area.

Data would be fed back into UKADGE and NADGE by mobile microwave, troposcatter or a Land Rover-towed satellite terminal. To ensure destruction of these mobile radars the USSR would be likely to target the area with large dirty warheads.

Data from Buchan are transmitted to the rest of UKADGE and NADGE by a microwave link to the ACE HIGH station on Mormond Hill, and probably also by landline and subsea cables.

Buchan operates in the following way: once it or another radar station detects a target, this is reported to the UK Air Defence Data Centre, West Drayton, which checks the information against known movements of civil and military aircraft. If it cannot be identified from these, the information is passed to the Air Defence Operations Centre at High Wycombe, where the decision to 'scramble' fighters is made. The HQ 11 Group at RAF Bentley Priory then allocates particular fighter units to the task. The interceptors (usually Phantoms from Leuchars) are then vectored to their target by Buchan, other UKADGE/NADGE radar stations such as Saxa Vord, or c^3i aircraft such as the Nimrod AEW.3.

Great play is made by the RAF about the role of UKADGE in intercepting Soviet 'bombers' off Britain, but it has been officially stated that no Soviet military aircraft has ever penetrated UK airspace.[32] Many of the intercepted aircraft are off-course commercial aircraft, while most of the rest are not 'bombers' but intelligence-gathering and maritime patrol aircraft such as the Bear and Badger. Suggestions that the number of these interceptions is steadily increasing do not stand up under scrutiny. The official figure for 1980 was five Soviet aircraft intercepted a week,[33] while in 1982 an RAF statement put the figure at four a week, and Saxa Vord, the prime front-line UK radar station, deals with fewer than two a week.[34]

In spring 1983 work started on an £8 million redevelopment of RAF Buchan's accommodation site at Boddam village. This is likely to lead to an increase in personnel beyond the current complement of over 400.

80. Clochandighter, Aberdeen   Microwave relay station in the US navy's UKMS.

81. Craigiebarns House, Dundee   The HQ of Caledonian Sector of the UKWMO, controlling the five ROC groups in Scotland, including 28 Group which is also located here. Its task is to collate and distribute information on nuclear blast and fall-out levels throughout Scotland during a nuclear attack. The UKWMO bunker, 40 feet underground on two levels, was adapted from an RAF Fighter Control bunker in 1961. Also at Craigiebarns House is the wartime headquarters of Tayside Regional Council. In 1981 this had, like many local authority bunkers, very few facilities – not even a telephone – in stark contrast to the heavily-equipped UKWMO bunker next door.

82. Craigowl Hill, Dundee   Since 1963 this British Telecom (BT) microwave relay station has illegally, but with the full connivance of BT, provided the US intelligence-gathering organisation, the National Security Agency (NSA), with access to private and commercial international telephone and telegraph cables which make a landfall in Scotland. These are from and to Canada, Norway, Iceland and the Faeroes. These cables also feed into the domestic telephone network.

The southward link from Craigowl Hill is known as 'Northern Backbone'. It provides 3,840 lines from Craigowl via the BT microwave network to a tower at Hunter's Stones near Harrogate. From there a 'private' cable runs into the NSA's huge eavesdropping station at Menwith Hill. Campbell has described this installation's bugging activities.[35]

The revelation of Craigowl's links to the NSA in 1980 created a public outcry. Questions were asked in the House and the local MP and Dundee District Council made attempts to have the station's function clarified by the Post Office (now BT), the MOD, the Scottish Office and the Secretary of State, but all stonewalled the questions and refused to discuss the matter. There were, however, no denials of the base's role.

Craigowl Hill is also a link in the US navy's UKMS microwave chain, although it seems that this and other UKMS stations south of Kinnaber have been disused since 1978. Also at Craigowl is a NATS VHF/UHF radio relay for communication with civil and military aircraft.

British Telecom communications networks

Civil telecommunications systems are widely used for military purposes
and the British Telecom (BT) network is no exception to this. It is used
by the military to increase 'redundancy' and disperse lines of communication. Laurie has shown how the BT trunk telephone network is
hardened against nuclear effects and is routed around likely targets.[36]
BT also runs a number of back-up communication systems which would
be used by the state in periods of emergency government such as prior
to a nuclear war. These are in addition to the Scottish Home and
Health Department's extensive point-to-point radio system.

The BT microwave radio network is now a prominent feature of the
Scottish landscape. Its steel towers, with dish, drum and horn aerials
mounted on them, are situated 12–50 miles apart. The origins of this
system are shrouded in mystery but Laurie and Campbell seem to have
established that work began in the 1950s as part of an update of the
UK's military radar system, which required greater data transmission
capacity than was available from landlines. The resulting microwave
network, known as 'Backbone', was rebuilt in the 1960s when a further
revamping of the military radar system was under way and a new phase
of civil defence spending was initiated. Two years before completion of
this network, a new high-capacity link was established with the sole
purpose of allowing the US National Security Agency (NSA) to tap
international telephone and telegraph lines running through Britain.

Microwave systems have several advantages for the state and the
military over other systems, particularly in times of 'civil unrest'. It is
much easier to guard a few steel towers than hundreds of miles of
underground cable. Microwave aerials are highly mobile and can be set
up very quickly; they are a relatively cheap way of communicating
large amounts of data across inhospitable terrain or water.

In wartime microwaves would be vulnerable to jamming, interception and nuclear effects. The USA has operated SIGINT satellites for
some time which collect stray microwave signals from above the USSR
and elsewhere, and the USSR is likely to have a similar facility. Though
Laurie claims that microwave towers are built to withstand a 5 megaton
explosion four miles away, it is highly unlikely that the BT network
would survive a nuclear attack.

The BT microwave system not only transmits military radar data
from radar stations to command centres, but carries much of the armed

forces' day-to-day message traffic as well as an increasing proportion of trunk telephone traffic. It also carries colour TV signals to transmitter masts and is used for transmission of oil/gas and other telemetry traffic. Microwave networks are also operated by the two Scottish Electricity Boards and Scottish Gas. There may be plans to take these over for military use in wartime, although the MOD now has its own microwave network, called BOXER, for predominantly peacetime use, and a point-to-point VHF/UHF radio system called MOULD which would be used for military emergency government.

---

83. Crimond, Aberdeenshire An RN/NATO communications station, opened in 1978 after expenditure of £8 million and amidst great concern that its powerful radio signals might interfere with control systems or cause a gas explosion at the nearby St Fergus gas terminal. At one point the MOD was considering closing Crimond completely and was looking for an alternative site in Easter Ross. Following MOD claims that the site was the optimum UK location for such a station, and despite some parties' continued doubts about safety, the station has continued operations.

Crimond's function is to provide naval communications for the North Atlantic and North Sea, using 3 LF and 13 HF transmitters and a variety of aerial masts up to 900 feet high. The LF transmissions not only overcome some of the limitatons of HF propagation in northern regions but enable Crimond to transmit signals to nuclear submarines trailing an aerial near the surface. The HF networks provide two-way ship-to-shore as well as broadcast facilities, with Crimond relaying messages between command centres and ships. In 1981 Crimond was described as a 'vital communications centre linking ships and aircraft to one another and to Pitreavie nerve centre'[37] which suggests that Crimond is one of the northern pair of stations in the MATELO system (the other being Milltown). Crimond has a large log periodic steerable 'fishbone' aerial which is used to receive faint HF signals from distant ships and maritime patrol aircraft.

84. Cultybraggan, Perthshire Army training camp, used by a wide variety of regular and TAVR units from all over Scotland.

Field training is carried out in the nearby Tighnablair training area.

85. Dundee TAVR units here are a Blowpipe anti-aircraft missile troop of 212 (Highland) Light Air Defence Battery, Royal Artillery (v); 117 (Highland) Field Support Squadron, Royal Engineers (v); 2 Squadron, 39th (City of London) Signal Regiment (v), which is assigned direct to HQ UK Land Forces for home defence tasks; A Company, 1st Battalion 51st Highland Volunteers, and 225 (Highland) Field Ambulance, RAMC (v).

In 1981 the latter unit co-sponsored a conference in Ninewells Hospital entitled 'Coping with the Holocaust' in an effort to get medical staff sufficiently interested in treating the victims of nuclear war to join the TAVR Medical Corps. The conference was cancelled on the orders of HQ Army Scotland on the grounds that it was 'too sensitive' an issue for the army to be involved in.

Also in Dundee are the Tay Division of the RN reserve whose part-time members train on an inshore minesweeper, a REME Contract Repair Branch which maintains army vehicles in the area, an MOD Personnel Selection Office and an Inspector of Stores and Clothing from the MOD Quality Assurance Directorate who oversees MOD contracts in local factories.

86. Edzell, Angus This is probably the base in Scotland which the USA would least wish to lose. It was an RAF airfield until 1958 and nominally remains an RAF base. The USAF had a 'radio facility' here from 1951 to 1955 which may have engaged in SIGINT and transmitter location in conjunction with the former USAF/US Army Security Agency base at Kirknewton. The US navy arrived in 1960, since when Edzell has been known as a US Naval Security Group Activity (NSGA). The Naval Security Group is just one component of the huge intelligence-gathering organisation, the NSA, which provides the USA with 80 per cent of its intelligence data from some 2,000 listening stations worldwide. SIGINT 'in the field' is collected for the NSA by military personnel of the service cryptologic agencies – not only the NSG but the Army Security Agency and the Air Force Security Service. NSA's international 'tapping' with the conni-

vance of British Telecom has been amply described by
Campbell.[38] Edzell is the only Scottish NSA base, though the NSA
does have close links with GCHQ, its British equivalent.

Edzell must be of particular importance to the USA due to the
Norwegian government's reluctance to permit such US-operated
bases on Norwegian soil and the acquiescent attitude of
Whitehall to US bases.

Edzell has over 620 military and more than 260 civilian
personnel. The latter are believed to be largely NSA cryptana-
lysts who operate the most secret devices in the operations
centre. This centre is occupied by over 140 people at a time and
contains more than $40 million-worth of equipment. This large
number of US personnel and their dependants are mainly
housed in a mini-Middle America built inside the base. There is
a Department of Defense School and acres of housing. The old
RAF hangars have been converted into theatres, cinemas, gyms,
shops, hobby workshops, etc., which help to reduce daily
contact with the locals. Security at the main gate is looked after
by British MOD police but internal security is performed by
Company B, Marine Support Battalion, whose personnel carry
out 'rapid deployment during contingencies',[39] i.e. they would
forcibly take over Edzell town and its environs.

Edzell engages in a number of activities, which neither fulfil
what might be termed a 'NATO function' nor contribute to the
defence of the UK. The official guide for new Edzell personnel
states that the base's mission is to:

> operate an HF DF facility and provide communications and
> related support, including communications relay, com-
> munications security and communications manpower assist-
> ance to navy and other Dept. of Defense elements within the
> area [the north-east Atlantic]; to serve as an efficient instru-
> ment of US foreign policy by initiating and continuing action
> programs which promote positive relations between [the
> base] and foreign nationals [that's us], and which assist
> individual naval personnel and their families to work effec-
> tively, live with dignity and satisfaction and function as
> positive representatives of the navy and of the United States
> while overseas.[40]

To be rather more to the point, Edzell is believed to carry out the following functions:

(a) Direction-finding (DF) of Warsaw Pact and other radio transmitters, and SIGINT-gathering, both by means of the huge 500 metre diameter, 20 metre high, AN/FLR-12 circular antenna which is prominently located with an integral operations centre, and microwave link through the UKMS to Kinnaber, on one of the old runways.

Edzell's HF direction-finding function is part of a worldwide system known as 'Project Bullseye', which is concerned with tracking Soviet naval forces by intercepting their HF and possibly low-VHF radio transmissions. The USA has participated in a joint ocean DF-monitoring network with the UK, Canada and Australia since 1973. A more recently-installed system at Edzell, known as Classic Wizard, operates on a worldwide basis and has been referred to in US Congress documents as being present at seven other US navy bases worldwide besides Edzell.[41] None of these is in north-west Europe, though there is an NSG SIGINT station at Keflavik, Iceland. Certainly there are DF bases in Norway operated by Norwegian Military Intelligence. It is likely that Edzell performs functions considered too sensitive to be performed by US nominees, although conceivably Norway, with its policy of not allowing permanent stationing of foreign troops in peacetime, might classify NSA agents as 'non-military'. Edzell's occupants can often be seen around the north-east wearing their 'NSG–Sinop' (another US spy base in Turkey) emblazoned windcheaters and heard spouting out the rigours of duty tours at Diego Garcia in the Indian Ocean.

A satcom dish can be seen on the top of the operations block in the middle of the circular aerial. This may be for real-time co-operation work with the other Classic Wizard or DF bases, such as those in Norway or at Keflavik. Presumably, as Ocean Surveillance Satellites become operational, this equipment will be directed more towards its original role of locating and intercepting ground transmitters and their signals, especially for updating the SIOP nuclear target list. In keeping with US tradition, Edzell may also be engaged in intercepting British, NATO and neutral countries' military and diplomatic signals. It is probably not working on electronic espionage against the Scottish populace (that can be done elsewhere) though the base does take more than a passing interest in peace protestors.

(b) Being relatively flat, electronically 'known' and fairly interference free, Edzell is an ideal site for satellite ground terminals (SGTs), of which it has five plus the one mentioned above. There are a number of functions which these may perform; the most likely tasks are:

(i) The relay of real-time intelligence data back to the USA, especially to the NSA's HQ at Fort Meade, Maryland, via the DSCS (see West Murkle).

(ii) Real-time control of US 'ferret' satellites by means of the Satellite Data System (SDS) which coincidentally carries missile early-warning sensors and AFSATCOM transmitter/receivers mounted 'piggy-back' to give extra radio links to US nuclear bombers and SSBNs in the Northern Waters area. This former function may well be operated in conjunction with Project Bullseye and/or Classic Wizard.

(iii) SDS also acts as a 'ferret' in Molniya (i.e. circum-polar) orbit which takes them over the northern USSR; they may 'dump' stored electronic data as they pass over Edzell.

(iv) Edzell may be far enough north to eavesdrop on transmissions from Soviet communications satellites in Molniya orbit; this SIGINT data would then be analysed and/or relayed over to the USA.

Ocean surveillance satellites

The USA has been active in the field of ocean surveillance satellites (OSSS) since 1965. In 1971 three satellites were launched on one rocket and successfully demonstrated all-weather real-time mapping of all Soviet surface vessels. The object of this was to provide data for guiding surface-to-surface missiles to their targets. Two 'Big Bird' close-look satellites launched in 1975 were for ocean surveillance purposes. These preceded the first launches in the 'White Cloud' series which is believed to operate at Edzell. The Naval Ocean Surveillance Satellite launched in 1976 carried three sub-satellites which operate with a 'mother' satellite to maximise coverage over the Pacific. Its

Atlantic counterpart was launched in 1977. These electronic intelligence ocean reconnaissance satellites (EORSATS) or 'ferrets' monitor the location of surface vessels by detecting ship-borne radar and radio emissions. The system became fully operational in 1980.

The latest US OSS development is the 50 per cent civil-funded National Oceanic Satellite System (NOSS). It will be launched by the space shuttle and be recoverable from orbit for maintenance and relaunch. Amongst its other functions, NOSS will be used to detect submerged submarines by sensing changes in the temperature of the ocean surface. Apparently related to NOSS is 'Clipper Bow' which was put into full-scale development in 1979 and is to be operational by 1985. It will also be put into orbit by the space shuttle. 'Clipper Bow' is an advanced system of satellite-borne high resolution radars which can detect and accurately locate surface vessels, including those maintaining radio silence, continuously, in all weathers, and in real time. Planned expansion at Edzell is believed to be connected with Clipper Bow.

With electronic emissions monitored by White Cloud and radar pictures received from Clipper Bow, the US navy will be able to track all naval vessels worldwide in real time.

The USSR has apparently fallen behind in OSS technology. Between 1969 and 1979 their OSSS operated in pairs for only 60 days a year. They suffered a major setback in 1978 when a nuclear-powered OSS developed a fault and crashed back to Earth, showering radioactive debris over north-west Canada. The USSR has now resumed its OSS programme and has at least one 'ferret'/radar satellite combination in orbit.[42] The USA believes that this limited system could provide target data for Soviet attacks on US naval forces. Soviet OSSS are now priority targets for US anti-satellite weapons. The converse is presumably true of US OSSS and their ground stations.

Like many other surveillance systems, OSSS are essential to 'counterforce' nuclear war. However, the increasing vulnerability of satellites to anti-satellite weapons may create pressures for a 'use 'em or lose 'em' approach to the targeting of Soviet naval vessels by OSSS.

(v) The two white 'golf-ball'-covered SGTS beside the public road at the south-west corner of the base, built in 1979/80, are believed to be for the control of, and receipt of data from, White Cloud/NOSS (National Oceanic Satellite System) satellites. Data on Soviet ships derived from these OSSS and Classic

Wizard may be passed first to the NSA or direct to the OSIS (Ocean Surveillance Information System). As at other NSG bases worldwide, Edzell's ocean surveillance buildings have recently been extended and their equipment upgraded. More than 100 extra military personnel are planned to be based at Edzell by 1986/87[43] and it is more than likely that they will be operating the new Clipper Bow radar OSS.

(vi) Edzell probably relays target data, derived from the various systems described above, to US ships and submarines by FLTSATCOM. This is probably part of 'Outlaw Shark'.

(c) Personnel maintain the UKMS southwards from the base. This is an important asset to the NSG, allowing direct secure high-capacity data links northwards as far as West Murkle and from there outwards by other means. No other location in Europe is known to have facilities such as those at Edzell. The base makes that area one of the prime targets for Soviet warheads in the event of war, while Classic Wizard and White Cloud would be essential tools in a US 'limited nuclear war'.

87. Elgin, Moray   TAVR infantry, HQ 2nd Battalion, 51st Highland Volunteers.

88. Fraserburgh Lighthouse, Aberdeenshire   MOD (Air) collecting centre, believed to be for collection of meteorological data for the military and possibly other users.

89. Inverbervie, Angus   US navy UKMS microwave relay, linking Kinnaber and Clochandighter.

90. Invergowrie, Dundee   D Squadron, 23 SAS (Special Air Service) Regiment, TAVR. This is one of two TAVR SAS units in Scotland. In 1980 the commanding officer of D Squadron was hoping to set up other SAS units in Aberdeen or Forfar as part of a publicity drive. It was also aimed to establish similar units in Edinburgh and Fife. Each SAS squadron has 15–20 men. Much of D Squadron's training is done at Barry Buddon.

91. Keith, Banffshire   TAVR infantry – a platoon of HQ Company, 3rd Battalion 51st Highland Volunteers.

92. Kinloss, Moray   The RAF's principal anti-submarine warfare (ASW) base. Since 1970 it has housed three of the RAF's four squadrons of Nimrod maritime patrol/anti-submarine aircraft.

The RAF's Nimrods are pooled on a 'wing' basis. The Kinloss Wing generally has about 18–20 aircraft available while each of the three squadrons has eight full 13 man crews.

Kinloss's main military task is the surveillance of Soviet ships and submarines, preparation for war against them, and support for the RN and other NATO surface fleets. In 1982 an award 'for advances in operational tactics'[44] was given jointly to 120 Squadron at Kinloss and 12 Squadron, which operates Buccaneers from Lossiemouth. This shows that Nimrods are used for the command and control of anti-shipping strikes by other aircraft.

Conventional weapons carried by the Nimrod include American Mk.46 torpedoes and, from 1982, the Marconi Stingray torpedo. Since the Falklands war Nimrods also have provision for Harpoon anti-ship and Sidewinder anti-aircraft missiles. The latter would be used to shoot down enemy maritime patrol or electronic intelligence aircraft. The RAF does not use the Nimrod's capacity to carry mines and conventional depth charges[45] but the American B-57 or Mk.101 nuclear depth bomb (NDB) is regarded as a standard weapon, having been first deployed on the Nimrod's predecessor, the Shackleton MR.3. Evidence of a nuclear weapons store at Kinloss is inconclusive, and there is no sign that Kinloss has any of the US personnel who would be necessary to operate the 'dual key' arrangements for these weapons. It is likely that all NDBs for Kinloss Nimrods are stored in the US navy nuclear weapons facility at Machrihanish, while others are stored at a similar facility at the RAF's other Nimrod base at St Mawgan, Cornwall. Kinloss Wing Nimrods are among the most regular visitors to Machrihanish.

The RAF's Nimrods are operated in peacetime by 18 (Maritime) Group, which shares the Northwood bunker with various naval commands. Allocation of tasks and operational control are exercised through HQ NORMAR at Pitreavie. Kinloss Nimrods operate worldwide but their main concern is the northeastern Atlantic and the Norwegian Sea, probably operating as far east as 30° east off north Norway. In wartime, Nimrods would be under the NATO command of CINCEASTLANT (Commander-in-Chief Eastern Atlantic), exercised through COM-

MAIRNORLANT at Pitreavie.

Kinloss Nimrods are also engaged in electronic warfare and electronic intelligence activities. In 1981, 120 Squadron won an award for the 'best contribution to the enhancement of the RAF's electronic warfare capability in that year.'[46] Nimrod MR.2s are expected to take over some of the electronic intelligence duties of the RAF's three Nimrod R.1s in future, so they will be taking on a more provocative role.

In addition to their purely military role Kinloss's Nimrods also carry out search and rescue duties, and surveillance of the UK's 200 mile exclusive economic zone. The latter duty, known as 'Offshore Tapestry', involves surveillance of oil and gas installations (paid for by the Department of Energy) and searching for boats fishing illegally in UK waters, on behalf of the Department of Agriculture and Fisheries for Scotland and the Ministry of Agriculture, Fisheries and Food. It costs nearly £2,000 per hour to fly these missions with a sophisticated aircraft like the Nimrod, and the practical results are open to question: the navy boarded 1,508 fishing vessels in 1980 but only just over 1 per cent of these boardings resulted in convictions for contravening regulations.[47] About 180 hours a month are spent by the RAF's Nimrods flying 'Tapestry' missions. They are regarded as a useful means of getting extra flying practice at reduced cost.

Kinloss also houses a wide variety of support organisations. The biggest of these is the Nimrod Major Servicing Unit (NMSU) which carries out major overhauls on all the RAF's 48 Nimrods (including, from 1984, the AEW.3s) at a rate of up to four at a time or around twelve a year. Others are the Nimrod Servicing School (which trains all Nimrod ground crew), the Air Engineering Development Team, the Nimrod Software Team, and part of the Maritime Patrol Cell of the Central Tactics and Trials Organisation.

An HF radio site on the north side of the airfield, part of the 'Flight Following System', is operated by 81 Signals Unit, which also runs the MATELO and STCICS communications systems at Milltown. Until early 1984 Kinloss also houses 236 Operational Conversion Unit (OCU), the Nimrod training unit, during conversion to the Nimrod MR.2. Kinloss also has a Mountain Rescue Team, and has administrative responsibilities for RAF Stornoway, RAF Alness, the RAF Adventure Training Centre at Grantown and part of Tain bombing range. Kinloss is also used by detachments of target-towing Canberras from 100 Squadron; these operate mainly with the South Uist missile range.

In 1982–83 a £2.2 million bulk fuel installation was built at Kinloss to provide forward operating base facilities for the Nimrod AEW.3s, due to enter service at Waddington, Lincolnshire in 1984. With about half of the RAF's total Nimrod force on the station, Kinloss would be a major Soviet target in wartime. In recognition of this there are plans to establish detachments of the RAF Regiment Rapier anti-aircraft missile and ground defence units from Lossiemouth at Kinloss in 1983–84.

Kinloss is also very frequently visited by other NATO anti-submarine aircraft, particularly during the three or four NATO maritime exercises every year.

93. Kinnaber, Angus Microwave relay station in the US navy's UKMS, linking Inverbervie to Edzell. The southward link to Craigowl Hill and beyond is believed to be disused.

94. Lossiemouth, Moray This RAF airfield was described in mid-1983 as 'Britain's most important front line station'.[48] There are units here from all four of the operational groups in RAF Strike Command, and the airfield is regularly used by a wide range of other RAF and NATO aircraft. The units based at Lossiemouth are:

(a) 12 Squadron, with up to 18 Buccaneers. Their role is to attack surface shipping using Martel (and from 1985, Sea Eagle) missiles, conventional or nuclear bombs, and rockets.

(b) 208 Squadron, with around a dozen Buccaneers. This unit, which was assigned to conventional and nuclear strike operations against land targets in the Allied Forces Northern Europe (AFNORTH) area – Norway and Denmark – moved to Lossiemouth from Honington, Suffolk, in summer 1983. It has now joined 12 Squadron in the anti-ship role.

(c) 226 Operational Conversion Unit (OCU), with 25 Jaguars. This unit trains all RAF Jaguar pilots before posting to operational squadrons, and has also trained Omani, Ecuadorian and Indian Jaguar pilots. The main RAF Jaguar force is based in Germany and has a nuclear capability. Its role is to strike airfields and 'second echelon' targets behind the front line. The 226 OCU trains pilots in nuclear bombing techniques such as 'toss' delivery. The unit's instructors would be sent to Germany in wartime to replace pilots killed in combat. The 226 OCU is likely to run down from 1986 as Jaguars in Germany are replaced by Tornados.

(d) 8 Squadron, with six ageing Shackleton AEW.2s. Their role is to extend air defence radar coverage by using their early warning radar to detect enemy aircraft beyond and below the coverage of shore-based radar stations. Fighter controllers aboard the aircraft direct interceptions by RAF Phantoms and others. This squadron will leave Lossiemouth in 1985 when the Nimrod AEW.3 becomes fully operational at Waddington, Lincolnshire. No. 8 Squadron also has a secondary offensive role, directing air attacks by 12 Squadron Buccaneers on surface ships.

(e) D Flight 202 Squadron, with two Sea King HAR.3 search and rescue helicopters.

(f) 48 Squadron RAF Regiment, with 12 Rapier surface-to-air missile launchers, for short-range air defence of the airfield. The unit's unofficial motto is 'If it flies, it dies'.

(g) 2622 (Highland) Squadron, Royal Auxiliary Air Force Regiment, a reservist unit whose members can frequently be seen prowling in the woods around the airfield. Their task is to prevent infiltration of the base by saboteurs. Ex-Minister of Sport Sir Hector Munro is the unit's Honorary Air Commodore.

Under plans announced in spring 1983 Lossiemouth will eventually become the base of all RAF Buccaneer operations. The Buccaneer training unit, 237 OCU, will move its 10 Buccaneers and several Hunters up from Honington early in 1984, and later that year one of the two Buccaneer squadrons from Laarbruch in Germany will also move in. It seems likely that the latter unit will relinquish its Central Front role on moving to

Lossiemouth, and may be reassigned to AFNORTH to further expand NATO's offensive power on its northern flank. Lossiemouth will eventually house up to 50 Buccaneers.

Although the Jaguar OCU may leave Lossiemouth in the next few years, there are already plans to replace it with the Hawks of 1 Tactical Weapons Unit, which trains RAF pilots in weapons delivery and combat tactics.

All these developments will mean a considerable increase in the disturbance and danger caused by low-flying throughout the Highlands. An article in RAF News in May 1983 put this succinctly:

> On the face of it, low-flying in the Highlands of Scotland would appear to be a suicidal enterprise, but . . . Lossiemouth is fast becoming a mecca for fast jet aircrews anxious to polish their skills in the rugged local countryside . . . the sparse population means few complaints about low altitude manoeuvres.[49]

The expansion also involves a massive construction programme, much of it aimed at making the base 'survivable' in a limited war. In 1979–80 a new weapons store was built on the south side of the airfield. Despite the concentration of the RAF's nuclear-capable Buccaneers at Lossiemouth, this is not a nuclear weapons store. It is possible that the British nuclear bombs for use by Lossiemouth's Buccaneers are stored at nearby Kinloss. At the same time an aviation fuel pipeline was built from Inverness Harbour to Lossiemouth. This has replaced delivery of fuel by road tankers, eliminating the base's susceptibility to drivers' strikes. It also enhances the base's war-fighting capabilities since 'fuel pipelines are almost invulnerable to nuclear attack.'[50] Early in 1983 work started on a £70 million building programme at Lossiemouth. About £20 million of this will go on 22 hardened aircraft shelters, construction of which began on the west side of the airfield in early 1983. These will be capable of protecting all the base's Buccaneers against conventional bombs, fall-out and chemical or biological agents. Meanwhile McTay Engineering started an £800,000 extension to a Buccaneer support facility in February 1983, and plans are in hand to extend and modernise the barrack blocks and domestic facilities at the base.

As the most northerly operational RAF airfield in the UK, Lossiemouth would play a crucial role in any war operations in the North Atlantic. Aside from the base's attraction in peacetime to NATO offensive aircraft due to the close proximity of vast low-flying areas and three weapons ranges, Lossiemouth is regularly visited by aircraft with a vital part in command and control of war in the North Atlantic, including US navy EC-130Q 'TACAMO' aircraft and USAF E-3A AWACS.

A peace camp was set up outside RAF Lossiemouth in October 1982. Despite much harassment it was still in existence at the time of writing.

95. Milltown, Moray   RAF communications facility, located on a former 'satellite' airfield for Lossiemouth which was used for field exercises by RAF Harriers in the early 1970s.

Milltown is operated by 81 Signals Unit, whose domestic (and some operational) facilities are at Kinloss. This site was probably chosen because it was already MOD land, had known soil resistivity, etc., is close to related operational and domestic facilities at Kinloss and Lossiemouth and has large areas of flat land suitable for aerial arrays.

Milltown operates two major communications systems – MATELO (believed to be an acronym for Maritime Telecommunications Operation) and STCICS (RAF Strike Command Integrated Communications System). MATELO was developed by NATO to permit any NATO long-range maritime patrol aircraft equipped with MATELO gear to communicate by HF radio with any MATELO ground station. The latter then relays the message by teletype to the addressee, e.g. Pitreavie, Kinloss or Northwood. MATELO has 'a transmitting and receiving site in the south of the UK and a similar pair in the north',[51] providing 20 two-way channels. The southern pair includes RAF Bampton Castle near Oxford; the nothern pair is Milltown and, it is believed, Crimond. Additionally there are two main control centres which back each other up. One of these may be at Pitreavie. The UK elements of MATELO became operational in 1976.

Milltown has been the northern element of STCICS since late 1980. STCICS was developed for the RAF by Racal Electronics. It provides HF ground-to-air and ship-to-shore radio communications by voice and teletype. Its introduction was concurrent with the entry into service of the Nimrod MR.2, which has much-improved encrypted teletype and voice HF equipment. Tall HF masts and the steerable log periodic arrays used for receiving faint signals from distant aircraft are clearly visible from the road.

Further expansion of Milltown's communications systems is likely. NATO's HF Improvement Programme, the 'Cross Fox' network which is 'intended to link shore-based and fleet-based commands'[52] and the MOD's Project Uniter may relate to Milltown, with the aim of further integrating the war-fighting capabilities of c³i systems in NATO's Northern Region.

96. Montreathmont, Brechin Scottish Home and Health Department (SHHD) radio station. Unlike most stations in the home defence point-to-point radio network, this one is permanently manned by radio technicians and others. It may perform a monitoring function rather than simply being a radio relay.

97. Montrose Airfield, Angus SHHD civil defence equipment store.

98. Mormond Hill, Aberdeenshire This installation, prominently located on a hilltop six miles south of Fraserburgh, has been described with some justification as 'the hub of military communications in Scotland.'[53] It has three main systems:

(a) The USAF North Atlantic Relay System (NARS). This is a 'souped-up' longer-range version of troposcatter radio, known as forward ionospheric scatter. It uses the huge square 'billboard' aerials at the west end of the site. NARS is used to relay strategic surveillance data from the BMEWS radar at Fylingdales, Yorkshire, via Mormond Hill to Stremoy (Faeroes), thence by Greenland and Canada to the USA. NARS was also designed to relay undersea surveillance data from and to the Fleet Ocean Surveillance Information Centre (FOSIC) in London, and is believed to transmit radar data from NADGE back to the US Air Defense Command (NORAD) bunker in Colorado.

(b) NATO's ACE HIGH. Radar data and communications from RAF Buchan are fed to and from the rest of the UKADGE and NADGE radar networks by a microwave link to the ACE HIGH network at Mormond Hill. Mormond Hill provides the tropo-scatter link between Mossy Hill in Shetland and the station in Northumberland serving RAF Boulmer radar station. The ACE HIGH aerials are the saucer-shaped, 60 ft diameter dishes at the east end of the hill.

(c) The US navy's US Microwave System (UKMS). Two micro-wave dishes on a tall thin mast between the NARS aerials link Clochandighter with Latheron in Caithness, passing target data on Soviet naval vessels from Edzell to Thurso, for communica-tion to US naval forces.

Mormond Hill's facilities would be vital elements in US and NATO plans for the use of nuclear weapons, not only for relaying warning data but also in controlling NATO's own forces. It would be an early target in any war.

The NATO Integrated Communications System (NICS)

NICS is the largest project funded under the NATO Infrastructure Programme, 'emphasising the high level of importance placed by NATO members on the need for effective and fully interoperable c^3.'[54] It was started in 1971 and is being built in two phases, the first of which is virtually complete. Phase II, to be complete by 1985, will be in four steps, emphasising 'survivability' and 'interoperability'.

NICS will use a 'meshed grid type common user network for voice, telegraph and data', i.e. it will be a highly automated, secure and survivable network using numerous transmission methods and routes round likely targets, linking NATO HQS, major commands, govern-ments and the US Defense Communication System. NICS is vital to the operation of systems such as NADGE.

The major elements of NICS Phase I are as follows:

(i) Existing systems in use within NATO, such as ACE HIGH, airborne relay, VHF/UHF, HF, LF, cable, microwave radio and civil telecom-munications. The latter carry about a third of NATO message traffic.

(ii) The Initial Voice Switched Network (IVSN), to provide 9,000 telephone connections within NATO by 1985. This will be overlaid on national systems (such as British Telecom) and will incorporate an existing secure voice network.

(iii) Telegraphic Automatic Relay Equipment (TARE). This will provide the largest automatic message processing and sorting system in the world. TARE was installed at Pitreavie in 1982.

(iv) Telecommunications Automatic Switching System (TASS). This provides a NATO-wide automatic telephone network.

(v) NATO III Satellite Subsystem. NATO already has three communications satellites in orbit. This project increases the number of fixed satellite ground terminals from 9 to 21. One of the new terminals is at Balado Bridge. A fourth part of this subsystem is intended to bestow greater physical and electronic security on the system in the 'unfriendly environment of . . . nuclear warfare.'[55]

NICS is swallowing $600 million in Phase I alone, which has involved work at 300 sites in Europe.

Although now functioning within the NATO Integrated Communications System, ACE HIGH was originally the main long-range communication system for relaying signals to initiate and co-ordinate the nuclear 'tripwire response' or 'massive retaliation' which was the strategy of the time. The system was completed in 1963. Since then it has been upgraded to adapt it to the much greater requirements of 'flexible response'. ACE HIGH provides 60 voice channels or 1,080 teletype channels, and links radar stations and command centres throughout Europe from north Norway to eastern Turkey. Five of the system's 90 stations are in Scotland (Saxa Vord, Collafirth Hill and Mossy Hill in Shetland; Mormond Hill and Buchan in Aberdeenshire). These are operated by the British army's 22nd Signals Squadron.

Physical protection of the ACE HIGH facilities is provided by armed RAF police and their dogs. The NARS facilities are guarded by USAF troops who apparently live a troglodytic existence under the hill.

99. Perth The HQ of 51 Highland Brigade, which controls all army units north of a line from Fife Ness to the Mull of Kintyre. TAVR units in Perth are the HQ of 1st Battalion 51st Highland Volunteers and 212 Ambulance Squadron, RCT (v). In September 1982 Perth became the base of one of the four new Home Service Force companies in the UK. This is a new Army reserve force tasked to guard key civil and military installations in wartime.

100. Perwinnes Hill, Dyce A NATS primary radar station which opened in 1976 with a Marconi s264A surveillance radar.

Data from here is relayed to the Scottish Air Traffic Control Centre at Prestwick, which is responsible for civil and military air traffic control over Scotland. Unfortunately the presence of this radar seems to have had no effect on the regular unauthorised and extremely dangerous breaches of busy civil airspace around Aberdeen by military aircraft in recent years.

101. Perwinnes Moss, Aberdeen   Training area for the heavy earth-moving vehicles of Plant Troop, 117 (Highland) Field Service Squadron, Royal Engineers (v).

102. Peterhead, Aberdeenshire   (a) Rifle range for personnel from RAF Buchan and (b) TAVR infantry, HQ 3rd Battalion 51st Highland Volunteers.

103. Rosehearty, Aberdeenshire   RAF bombing range, in use for over 30 years. Its main users are RAF Jaguars and Buccaneers and USAF F-111s, which drop 4 lb and 28 lb practice bombs on floating targets about half a mile off Dundarg Castle.

Frequently F-111s on their way south from here infringe civil airspace around Aberdeen, and in December 1979 a 48th TFW F-111 lobbed a 28 lb practice bomb on to Bankhead Farm. This led to the banning of toss-bombing manoeuvres at Rosehearty. A similar incident in the 1960s killed several animals in a barn. After the 1979 incident the farmer at Bankhead said:

> People here have been complaining for years about the annoyance caused by the planes but nothing has been done. They swoop low over the farms and houses every day and the noise is quite deafening.[56]

104. Tighnablair, Perthshire   Army training area of about 4,700 acres, used by units from Cultybraggan camp.

105. Whitestone, Dunblane   A 322 acre army rifle range used by regular units from Cultybraggan and local TAVR units.

106. Windyheads Hill, Aberdeenshire   NATS VHF/UHF radio relay station for air traffic control communications between civil and military aircraft and SCATCC Prestwick. The station's military functions may be increasing since RAF personnel were involved in construction work here in 1982.

Section four: West Central and South-west Scotland

107. Ardeer, Ayrshire   Nobel Explosives Co. Ltd explosives factory, a major supplier to the MOD.

108. Arrochar, Loch Long   An RN torpedo range. Royal Navy and other NATO submarines and surface ships practise torpedo firing in the whole of the northern half of Loch Long against four moored sonar targets. The range is controlled from a pier and buildings on the west side of Arrochar. Associated with this range is the 'Coulport Cableway', an installation adjacent to the nuclear weapons store further down the loch. The cableway can fire model torpedoes and test vehicles up to 1,000 lb in weight into the water at speeds of up to 300 m.p.h. at any angle from vertical to horizontal. Some of these models are caught in nets stretched across the loch. Others, such as the E1 test torpedo used in the development of the Marconi Spearfish, are tethered underwater during trials. The E1 was used in this way in trials on Loch Long from 1977 to 1979 'so that the propulsion system could be tested at high speeds.'[57]

109. Auchendennan, Loch Long   An RN oil fuel pipeline and pumping station.

110. Ayr   TAVR centre, infantry of B Company, 1st Battalion 52nd Lowland Volunteers, and FV721 Fox light armoured reconnaissance vehicles of A Squadron, The Queen's Own Yeomanry, Royal Armoured Corps (v).

111. Barnsford, Renfrewshire   102 (Clyde) Field Squadron, Royal Engineers (v), part of 71 Engineers Regiment, Glasgow.

112. Beith, Ayrshire   An RN armament depot. Believed to store a range of conventional armaments for Clyde-based ships and submarines.

113. Bishopton, Renfrewshire   This vast area near Glasgow airport houses a Royal Ordnance factory which is 'the UK's largest producer of propellants for use in gun ammunition, rockets and guided weapons. The sole UK manufacturer of combustible charge containers.'[58] Bishopton produces rocket fuel for Polaris, Lance, Sea Cat, Sea Wolf, Rapier and Martel missiles. The workforce numbers 2,300 but trends towards a 'more commercial environment' in the ROFs are likely to lead to

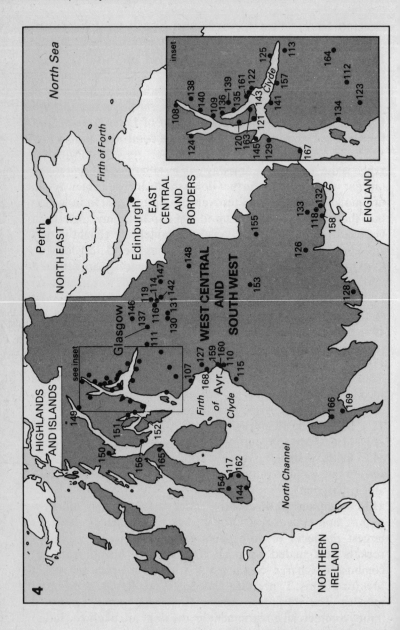

redundancies. Bishopton also houses the main Scottish labora-
tory of the MOD's Materials Quality Assurance Directorate.

114. Bothwell Haugh, Lanark   TAVR training area.

115. Browncarrick Hill, Girvan   Microwave relay site in the
UK navy's UKMS, linking Slieveanorra in Antrim with the UKMS
in Scotland. Browncarrick Hill has apparently been disused
since 1978 when the US navy abandoned their radio station near
Derry, but the aerials are still in place and the site is still leased
to the US navy.

116. Cambuslang (Dechmont), Lanarkshire   TAVR small-arms
range.

117. Campbeltown Loch, Kintyre   NATO POL depot, used by a
wide variety of NATO ships and diesel submarines, RFA vessels
and other military tankers, particularly during major NATO
maritime exercises.

118. Chapelcross, Dumfries-shire   British Nuclear Fuels Ltd
(BNFL) nuclear plant, opened in 1958 to produce weapons-grade
plutonium for British nuclear weapons, with electricity being
produced as a by-product. In 1980 a tritium plant was opened
here. This was built to reduce the UK's dependence on American sources of tritium for their bombs. Meanwhile BNFL's deal
for the exchange of British plutonium for US enriched uranium
and tritium has been extended to 1984. SIPRI has estimated that
the USA will require 10,000 or more new warheads for its new
nuclear weapons over the next 10 years;[59] this huge demand is
likely to filter through to the requirements for plutonium
production from plants such as Chapelcross.

119. Coatbridge, Lanarkshire   124 Field Squadron, Royal Engineers (V).

120. Coulport, Loch Long   An RN armament depot, built in
the mid-1960s to store, maintain and arm Polaris A3 missiles for
the four 'Resolution' class SSBNs based at nearby Faslane.

Before an SSBN returns to Faslane from its 60 day patrol it
berths at Coulport to unload its missiles. Each of the 'old'
Polaris missiles has three 150 kiloton warheads but the new
Chevaline Polaris has six 40 kiloton warheads and 'penetration
aids'.

At Coulport the warheads are separated from the missiles,

which are overhauled, tested and stored in underground chambers in the hillside. The process buildings can be clearly seen from Ardentinny on the other side of the loch.

Nuclear warheads require regular inspection, maintenance and overhaul and this means moving them from Coulport to the ROF at Burghfield near Reading. Until 1978 this was done by the RFA's armament-carrying vessels, routing through the Irish Sea, but fear of hijacking led to a transfer to rail and road. The rail convoys were revealed by Campbell in 1981,[60] while the road convoys came to light in April 1983 when a member of the Faslane Peace Camp made a brave effort to let down the tyres of a support vehicle. With the progressive introduction of Chevaline warheads from 1982 the frequency of the convoys has increased. At the time of writing they were running at least once a month, routing via the A74 and making an overnight stop at the army's Longtown armament depot near Carlisle. Security is provided by members of Commachio Company, Royal Marines and a special forces element of the RAF Regiment and RAF Provost and Security Service. The revelations about these convoys running through a declared nuclear-free zone prompted strong protests from Strathclyde Regional Council.

Chevaline

The Chevaline project was mooted by the project-hungry Atomic Weapons Research Establishment in 1967 and given the go-ahead by a top secret subcommittee in Heath's cabinet in 1970. At that time it was estimated to cost £175 million. Galloping costs and technical problems were concealed in subsequent Wilson, Callaghan and Thatcher annual military budgets, and no direct reference to Chevaline was made in parliament until January 1980, by which time it had cost £1,000 million and was having severe technical problems.

It is possible that Chevaline started out as a British MIRV project but scientists got out of their depth without US help and cash, so ended up settling for the 'poor man's MIRV' of MRVs plus counter-measures.

Chevaline's justification has been 'the Moscow criterion' – the USSR's development of an ABM system round Moscow had threatened the ability of Polaris to reach its target. This assumes that British

Polaris weapons are only targeted on Moscow (this is not the case) and that Britain would be firing nuclear weapons at the USSR without the USA using any of its weapons. Even before Chevaline had come into service, the government was using the same 'Moscow criterion' as a justification for Trident D5 – a system with the ability to hit at least eight times the number of targets.

The first Chevaline-equipped SSBN went on patrol in late 1982 but it will be 1988 before all four submarines are fitted out, since each vessel has to be modified when they come due for refit at Rosyth. Meanwhile a further £300 million is being spent on renewing the missiles' motors to make sure Britain can launch its contribution to the holocaust before the navy gets Trident.

Until recently most of the missile maintenance work at Coulport was done by about 750 civil servants, but the 1981 strike by 41 staff, amongst others, which 'halted all documentation for the regular replacement of newly serviced missiles on submarines'[61] has made the government rethink this policy. Mixed civil–military manning has since been introduced so that the navy can rearm and restock the SSBNs itself. This was probably the reason for the loss of 400 civilian jobs at the Clyde submarine base in 1982.

In May 1981 a delegation of MOD mandarins led by Lord Trenchard revealed the expansion plans for Coulport, to take the new Trident missile system, to an 'astounded' audience of local councillors and officials. Despite rumours that these developments might take place elsewhere, the people living on the Rosneath peninsula had expected new works for years. Work for Trident I facilities had actually started before the meeting.

Lord Trenchard revealed plans for a 10 fold expansion of Coulport from its present 294 acres to 2,894 acres, turning the entire peninsula into a military compound with a narrow civilian strip round the south-east side. There would be a new internal road system, process, storage and administration buildings, a jetty for the deeper draught Type 640 Trident submarines, security fences, etc. In May 1981 the cost of these works was put at £365 million, including a by-pass above some of the villages on the A833 road to the base. More recently this was modified to £500 million. Trenchard lectured the meeting that the development was 'essential for the country, good for Scotland and on balance good for the locality.'

Local authorities and other concerned bodies subsequently attempted to obtain further details of the MOD's sketchy plans. In particular, details of the 'yellow line' or 'inhabited building distance' were sought. Within this 'yellow line' area the MOD does not wish to see developments which could cause concentrations of people who would stand to be in greater danger than previously. Trenchard promised to supply these details, but the promise was an empty one. An MOD functionary at Faslane told council officials that the promise had been 'a mistake'. As a result the local authorities decided to have nothing further to do with the MOD, and adopted a policy of not co-operating. Since then they have given considerable support to the Anti-Trident Campaign.

In March 1982 the government announced their intention to buy the Trident II D5 instead of the C4 version. This will involve a major but as yet unspecified revision of the Coulport expansion plans. Nor is it clear how the September 1982 announcement that missile servicing will be done in the USA will affect Coulport.

The Trident D5 missile is considerably larger than the C4, and can carry up to 14 MIRVs as opposed to eight in the C4. The D5 will not be flight-tested by the USA until at least 1987. If the UK purchase proceeds, work at Coulport would not be completed until two or three years after the original 1989–90 projection. Site works are nevertheless proceeding; amongst the contractors at the Coulport site in 1983 was McTay Engineering.

The total cost of shore facilities for Trident at Coulport, Faslane and Rosyth has been conservatively put at some £650 million. Coulport still takes up the lion's share of this despite the announcement in September 1982 that, primarily for financial reasons, the D5 missile fitting and servicing would be carried out not at Coulport but at the US Navy Trident Atlantic Facility, King's Bay, Georgia.

The SSBNS would probably need to visit King's Bay twice every seven years (before and after every refit at Rosyth). The D5's systems are designed to enable the missile to remain inside its launch tube for the whole seven-year period, hence under normal circumstances the missiles would not be removed, serviced or stored at Coulport. There is, of course, a catch to this apparently good news. The warheads will, as before, be fitted and stored at Coulport, and it seems likely that some missiles might also be stored there for 'contingencies'. It appears that the land acquisitions and substantial site works will proceed much the same as planned.

One aspect of the original plans which must be brought to light is that Coulport may not even have conformed to the military's own safety limits for storing the Trident missile. This may explain the MOD's reluctance to reveal the 'yellow line'. In 1981 it was said that the 10 fold expansion of Coulport was needed because, for safety reasons, greater distances were required between the larger storage buildings for the more numerous and powerful Trident warheads, trigger explosives and, at that time, missile fuel. The government has said it does not wish to have more warheads in the Trident D5 force than are currently carried by Polaris. This would probably mean six MIRVS in a missile designed for fourteen. However, such self-restraint would be out of keeping with military tradition and the AWRE at Aldermaston will, out of self-interest, push for as complex a device as possible. At least eight MIRVS are therefore more likely. Consequently the land requirements at Coulport may have been even greater than it is physically possible to provide at this site. Since the safety figures are kept secret the truth may never be known.

The decision to service the D5 missiles in the USA is also politically undesirable from the government's point of view since it further undermines the notion of an 'independent' British strategic nuclear force. Fitting and servicing the D5 in the USA is therefore tacit recognition that Coulport is physically unsuitable for the navy's needs and nominal safety criteria. Indeed the MOD has declined invitations to state that Coulport would have met the D5's safety requirements. By contrast the announcement in 1980 of King's Bay, Georgia as the Atlantic Seaboard base for US navy Trident SSBNs:

> culminated the evaluation and analysis of many different base locations, operational capabilities and ability to satisfy the larger explosive arcs required by the more powerful propellant in the Trident C4 missile . . . King's Bay is the only base on the east coast with the required explosive handling arc for the current Trident C4 missile and any modernised missile contemplated.[62]

The nearest large town to King's Bay is Jacksonville, Florida, some 30 miles away. At Coulport there are over a million people within a similar distance.

Further dangers may arise from 'the barges in Finart Bay, Ardentinny, associated with the Polaris depot.'[63] These seem to contain radioactive waste from nuclear submarine reactors. The barges, which are only a short distance offshore, and usually unattended, are progressively filled up with material from Coulport, then periodically towed round to Faslane. The personnel working on the barges wear white anti-radiation suits, and local people enjoying summer night barbecues on the beach opposite the barges have had searchlights turned on them from MOD police launches patrolling in the bay.

Despite his success in completely ignoring the evidence of two other public inquiries into military developments in Scotland (see *Stornoway* and *Castlelaw Hill*) the Secretary of State for Scotland has steadfastly refused to hold an inquiry into the Coulport plans. In an attempt to expose this blatant disrespect for democracy Strathclyde Regional Council held their own inquiry into the Trident expansion in June 1983.

Also at Coulport is a special launcher for catapulting test torpedoes into the water (see *Arrochar*).

121. Cove, Kilcreggan RN Staff Training Centre.

122. Craigendoran, Helensburgh An RN degaussing range, for de-magnetising the hulls and equipment of naval vessels to prevent them from triggering off magnetic mines.

123. Dalry, Ayrshire TAVR centre, one troop of 251 Fuel Tanker Squadron, RCT(V).

124. Douglas Pier, Loch Goil Admiralty Marine Technology Establishment (AMTE) outstation, used for trials of torpedoes and underwater test vehicles on the noise range in Loch Goil, which is 'primarily for the routine measurement of noise emitted by naval vesssels and submarines, but . . . also used for other acoustic purposes.'[64] Loch Goil has been used for sonar research since 1942.

125. Dumbarton TAVR infantry, D Company, 3rd Battalion 51st Highland Volunteers.

126. Dumfries TAVR centre, infantry and Royal Military Police.

127. Dundonald, Ayrshire NATS VHF/UHF radio relay for civil and military air traffic control.

128. Dundrennan, Kirkcudbright Armament Wing of the Trials Branch of the Trials and Evaluation Division, Military Vehicles and Engineering Establishment. This is a range area covering nearly 5,000 acres over which all tank weapons can be fired. It employs 200 civilians.

According to the Nugent Report[65] the range is quite heavily used in testing the accuracy and effectiveness of armour and ammunition, fire control and night vision aids, etc. A danger area of some 120 square miles extends out into the Solway Firth. Recently this has been used in test firings of depleted uranium anti-tank ammunition into the Irish Sea.

129. Dunoon TAVR Medical Corps, a detachment of 205 (Scottish) General Hospital, RAMC(V).

130. East Kilbride (Calderglen) SHHD Western Zone Control wartime government bunker.

131. East Kilbride TAVR centre, vehicles of 222 Squadron RCT(V).

132. Eastriggs, Annan Army explosive ordnance depot covering 1,111 acres, responsible for storage, maintenance and issue of bulk explosives. The Nugent Report stated that in 1972–73 'under plans to rationalise ammunition storage in the UK, the holdings at Eastriggs will be transferred to other existing sites once suitable facilities have been built',[66] and recommended disposal of the site, but the depot appears to be still in use. Also at Eastriggs is a detachment of the RCT's railway staff who not only operate the on-site railway sidings but 'would take over some civilian railways in an emergency.'[67]

133. Ecclefechan, Dumfries TAVR rifle range.

134. Fairlie, Ayrshire NATO mooring and support depot, built between 1959 and 1963 as the shore base of a £3.2 million boom defence system to protect the Clyde submarine bases from enemy submarines and torpedoes. Fairlie has a 450 yd long pier with rail access and a substantial storage building.

The term 'boom defence' originally referred to underwater nets to physically stop submarines entering a harbour or port area. It is now thought to encompass underwater hydrophone systems as well. These locate hostile submarines by sonar detection. The Clyde is understood to have an extensive network of seabed sonars. Fairlie repairs and maintains this system with the aid of boom defence-assigned elements of the Royal Maritime Auxiliary Service from Greenock, and also maintains other naval installations such as mooring buoys.

Fairlie is also used by Glenlight Shipping Company coasters transferring supplies for Holy Loch and Machrihanish from US navy supply ships to road transport.

135. Faslane, Gare Loch The RN Clyde Submarine Base, HMS *Neptune*, commissioned in 1967 to support the Polaris SSBN fleet. Based here are the 10th Submarine Squadron, with four 'Resolution' class SSBNS, and the 3rd Submarine Squadron with three 'Valiant' class SSNS and three 'Oberon' class diesel patrol submarines. Also at Faslane is a little-known foreign military presence, in the shape of at least two Dutch navy diesel submarines which operate closely with the RN. Their peacetime roles are surveillance of Soviet vessels and acting as targets for NATO ASW training. Other units at Faslane include the RN Polaris School, Submarine Sea Training and a number of maintenance and support facilities including the floating dry dock AFD 60. Tugs, boom defence vessels and other RMAS boats are operated from Greenock but commanded and administered from Faslane.

The 10th Submarine Squadron maintains one, and sometimes two, SSBNS on 60 day patrol at all times. A third is under refit at Rosyth, while the fourth is at Faslane preparing for its next patrol. The warheads (and some of the missiles) are removed from each SSBN at Coulport before the vessel returns to Faslane at the end of a patrol, and similarly each SSBN moves from Faslane to Coulport to be armed before going out on patrol.

Faslane was originally a wartime port for US troop movements to Europe. In 1962 it became the base of Britain's first SSN, HMS *Dreadnought*, joining the diesel-powered submarines in the 3rd Submarine Squadron.

Expansion at Faslane is very likely even if Trident is cancelled. The RN's SSN fleet is currently being built up from 12 vessels to at least 17 by 1990, and in the late 1980s the 'Oberons' will be replaced by the new Type 2400 patrol submarine.

Furthermore, Nott's 1981 Defence Review placed a heavy emphasis on the use of submarines deployed well north in the Norwegian and Barents Seas to seal off the Kola bases and thereby prevent the Soviet Northern Fleet access to the Atlantic. This is one of the prime examples of Britain falling into line with the new offensive strategy being adopted by the US navy in these and other waters. Faslane will play a major role in this.

Several weapons developments are currently in progress which affect Faslane. In 1982 the first Sub-Harpoon underwater-launched anti-ship missiles were deployed on RN SSNs. These will replace 40 year old Mark 8 torpedoes (the kind used by the Faslane-based HMS *Conqueror* to sink the *General Belgrano* in the Falklands war). In the next few years SSNs will also have the Marconi Spearfish, a heavyweight anti-submarine torpedo with a range of 25 miles and capable of speeds up to 70 knots. These will also be carried on Polaris submarines. In 1982, the latter started to receive the first Polaris A3T ('Chevaline') warheads (see *Coulport*).

Faslane has about 3,500 naval personnel and a plethora of associated installations from Arrochar and Loch Fyne in the north to Prestwick in the south. Security at Faslane and Coulport is provided not only by MOD police but also by a detachment of Commachio Company Royal Marines, whose black-clad SBS-trained supermen can occasionally be seen throwing themselves into the Clyde from RAF Hercules in training to repel subversives.

Two other units are stationed at Faslane: the Torpedo Trials Unit of the Naval Weapons Trials Organisation, which uses the facilities of the various underwater trials ranges in nearby lochs; and one of the Institute of Naval Medicine's four Naval Emergency Monitoring Teams (NEMTS). These teams normally consist of an officer and three ratings from the RN Electrical Branch but include a health physicist and a nuclear-trained medical officer when fully operational. They are responsible for responding to 'either a nuclear submarine reactor accident or a nuclear weapon accident'.[68] The ability of four men to cope with such incidents is open to question.

136. Garelochhead   A 4,573 acre army training area, used for infantry field firing, assault landings, adventure training and parachute dropping. Units using the area are housed in the Greenfield training camp above Faslane Bay.

137. Glasgow   A large number of army, navy and MOD (PE) installations and offices are located in Glasgow, the latter being quality assurance overseers for the considerable range of naval shipbuilding and weapons production in the area. The regular army has offices in Montrose House, while TAVR units in the city are a battalion HQ and three companies of infantry, an air defence battery, a battalion HQ and two companies of 'Paras', a Signals Regiment HQ (believed to be asssigned to 'home defence'), an Engineer Regiment HQ, an RCT Regiment HQ, an RAMC General Hospital unit, an RAOC Ordnance Field Park unit and a University OTC. The Royal Marines, Royal Navy and RAF also have reserve units in Glasgow. Many of these, and several of the TAVR units, would be assigned to 'home defence' in an emergency, rounding up 'subversives' and keeping the population in its place.

In March 1983 the government began the transfer of some MOD administrative jobs from the south of England to Glasgow. This is a mini-version of a 6,000 job regional employment plan initiated by the previous Labour administration. Under present plans 1,520 jobs will be transferred to Glasgow by 1985–86, about a third of these in the field of service and civilian personnel management, others in fields such as defence equipment codification.

138. Glen Douglas Although commonly assumed to be the storage site for the Poseidon warheads from US navy SSBNs in the Holy Loch, there is no evidence that this NATO ammunition depot contains any nuclear weapons. In any case all US navy warheads and missiles at Holy Loch are held in the tender care of heavily armed US Marines aboard the USS *Hunley* and are never taken ashore.

The site was bought by the Admiralty in 1956 and funds from the NATO Infrastructure Programme used to build a 'conventional naval ammunition'[69] depot between 1961 and 1963, with rail access and underground storage caverns built into the hillside. In the late 1970s a NATO jetty was built at Glenmallan on Loch Long to serve Glen Douglas, with a new MOD road linking the two through Gleann Culanach.

Although used on a day-to-day basis by the RN, Glen Douglas accounts for about half of the munitions which the US navy has 'prepositioned in the UK for the fleet operating in the Norwegian Sea and in that area.'[70] This is thought to amount to over 20,000 metric tons of weapons, although even the US navy itself does not seem to know; in July 1982 it was revealed in US congressional hearings that despite a grand-sounding Conventional Ammunition Integrated Management System the US navy had lost count of its weapons stocks, and that a stock-taking of US navy ammunition stored at Glen Douglas would be complete in May 1983.[71]

In June 1982 the first section of a second security fence had been erected at Glen Douglas and the foundations of a new building laid in the centre of the site. These may merely be part of a general increase in security at military bases, but could represent the first stages in Glen Douglas being given a nuclear storage capability.

139. Glen Fruin (Strone), Garelochhead Admiralty Marine Technology Establishment outstation, involved primarily in trials and development of the water entry phase of air-launched torpedoes and other weapons and equipment. In the early 1960s Glen Fruin tested the underwater ejection seat for the Buccaneer aircraft. The main facility is a 150ft by 40ft by 30ft water-tank 'with the 150 by 40ft side almost entirely of glass to permit observation of the entry phase of catapult-launched models of torpedoes and other devices.'[72]

140. Glenmallan, Loch Long NATO jetty, built in the late 1970s to serve the Glen Douglas Ammunition Depot, to which it is connected by road. Armaments, primarily torpedoes, are transported here by the RMAS Armament Carrier vessels *Throsk* and *Kinterbury*.

141. Greenock Several naval facilities associated with the Clyde Submarine Base, the following being most important:

(a) Marine Services Clyde, responsible for operating the Royal Maritime Auxiliary Service tugs, torpedo recovery vessels, boom defence vessels and other boats which support RN operations in the Clyde. These operate from Great Harbour, but have been controlled from Faslane since 1 January 1983. They include the 2nd Boom Defence Squadron and the Clyde Mooring and Salvage Squadron.

(b) HMS *Dalriada*, HQ Unit of the Royal Naval Reserve (RNR), at the Navy Building at Fort Matilda. This is believed to function, amongst other things, as the command and control centre for the network of undersea hydrophones in the Clyde which detect and locate possible submarine threats to the two SSBN bases. This was revealed in late 1982 when a retiring member of the RNR staff at Greenock was described in the local press as one of a team of sonar operators.

(c) Greenock Harbour is used by coasters transporting supplies and garbage of all descriptions (including live ammunition, pornography and phials of chemicals) to and from the USS *Hunley* in Holy Loch. It would also be established in wartime as a US army/navy terminal for transatlantic troop reinforcements.

Greenock also has a Royal Marines Reserve detachment. The MOD (Air) Ocean Weather Ships Base at Greenock, which operated two converted frigates as Atlantic weather ships, closed in January 1982 with the loss of 50 shore jobs.

142. Hamilton, Lanarkshire The Regimental HQ of the Cameronians here has only administrative/ceremonial functions, but the town also houses two TAVR infantry companies from the 52nd Lowland Volunteers.

143. Helensburgh (Churchill Square) MOD (Navy) Provost HQ (i.e. police); also offices, stores and a housing estate for RN personnel.

144. High Keil, Southend, Kintyre Racal-Decca Hi-Fix/6 radio navigation transmitter station, for use in mine counter-measures in the Clyde approaches. (For further details see Ledaig, Barra.)

145. Holy Loch Without doubt the most infamous US base in Scotland, being the original focus of 'Ban the Bomb' campaigning in Scotland. Since March 1961 Holy Loch has been a Submarine Support Base for the US navy's 14th Submarine Squadron ('SubRon 14'), and is known as Submarine Refit Site One. The base was originally authorised by Prime Minister Macmillan as part of the abortive deal whereby the UK was to buy the Skybolt nuclear missile from the USA to arm Vulcan bombers. The USA needed a location like Holy Loch at the time due to the relatively short range of the early Polaris missiles (1,500 nautical miles for the A2) which necessitated patrols in the eastern Atlantic. Holy Loch has never been a NATO facility. It exists simply through bilateral agreement.

The base comprises sea and land components. The offshore part is where all the weapons are presently concentrated. It consists of:

(a) The 19,000 ton submarine tender USS *Hunley*.

(b) A large crane barge.

(c) The USS *Los Alamos*, an auxiliary floating dry dock, over 1,000ft long and with a lifting capacity of 40,000 tons. This has been at Holy Loch since 1961. It supports ballistic missile submarines 'at advanced bases . . . and . . . provides repair capabilities in forward combat areas.'[73] This enables SubRon 14 to be virtually self-sufficient.

(d) Three large harbour tugs and a fleet of smaller support vessels which are berthed alongside the crane barge and dry dock.

(e) Various barges which lie at the head of the Holy Loch. Some of these contain explosive ordnance and heavy tools but others may store 'low level' nuclear waste discharged from submarine reactors.

Other vessels visit from time to time. The coasters of the Glenlight Shipping Company are used to remove rubbish from the *Hunley* to a dump in Greenock, and also to transfer supplies between supply ships, Greenock, Holy Loch and the NATO pier at Fairlie. The monthly US navy Military Sealift Command 'T-AK' supply ship is the *Hunley*'s lifeline. It brings in over-hauled Poseidon missiles, Mk.48 torpedoes, dry goods, tools, spares, diesel, fuel oil and food from the USA. Other regular US navy visitors to Holy Loch include satellite tracking ships and submarine rescue vessels.

The shore base is centred on Ardnadam Pier, Sandbank, but the ever-expanding garrison is spread throughout Dunoon and its environs. About one-third of the habitable area of the Sandbank community is now used by the US navy. American facilities include a Naval Exchange (subsidised supermarket), medical and recreational facilities, supply and vehicle servicing depots, a Fleet Post Office, various other offices, and accom-modation for naval personnel and their dependants such as Eagle Court, Sandbank (known as 'the Reservation' to local people).

The official figure for the number of US navy personnel is 1,800, but the *Hunley* alone has a full operational complement of over 2,500, and the crews of SSBNs are not included in the figure. There are also some 2,000 US dependants. About 650 houses in the area are occupied by US personnel and their families, while another 100 live in Greenock. The base's recreational facilities have trebled in area while by contrast those available for locals and visitors have declined with the downturn in tourism. US sailors have 500 car parking spaces in Sandbank while the locals and tourists have none.

More than 20 years of US occupation have borne heavily on the area in social terms. The large number of bored single sailors in an alien country has raised crime levels, particularly rape, vehicle offences, drink and drugs. The *Hunley* carries two lawyers to deal with US sailors' offences 'on the beach', as Scotland is known to them. Drug abuse is a severe problem throughout the US military and the navy in particular. The *New Statesman* has revealed several such cases at Holy Loch, including an occasion when an SSBN crewman brought drugs into Holy Loch on board a nuclear missile submarine whose patrol had commenced in the USA.[74] Despite 'dope dog' patrols of the *Hunley* every few hours, drugs remain a problem. There are also now worries in the US navy that success in combating drug abuse will merely lead to a re-emergence of a severe alcohol problem. This is exacerbated by the availability of cheap drink at the base's Commissary Exchange.

The tensions of living and working at a base like Holy Loch have from time to time erupted into violence. In October 1982 there was a race riot, involving some 60 men, on board the crane barge. This had to be stamped on rapidly before it spread to the *Hunley*. Fights on shore are a regular occurrence.

SubRon 14 is equipped with 7–10 of the US navy's total of 19 Poseidon-armed Lafayette and Benjamin Franklin class SSBNs. To fill the temporary 'missile gap' caused by the rearming of another 12 vessels of these same classes with Trident I C4 missiles, each of the 16 Poseidon missiles carried in each submarine has been modified to carry up to 14 Mk.3 MIRVs each of 50 kilotons, instead of their usual 10 MIRVs. A single SSBN at Holy Loch may therefore carry as many as 224 warheads, each several times more powerful than the bombs dropped on Japan in 1945. As many as four SSBNs may commonly be seen berthed alongside the *Hunley* at one time.

SubRon 16 operated another 10 Poseidon SSBNs from Rota in Spain until 1979, when they moved back to King's Bay, Georgia. These vessels patrolled mainly in the Mediterranean. Shortly afterwards another SSBN base on the Pacific island of Guam was closed down, giving Holy Loch the dubious honour of being the only foreign SSBN base anywhere in the world.

Poseidon will eventually be replaced in the US navy by the Trident missile, carried in converted Poseidon boats and in the enormous new 'Ohio' class submarines. It had been thought that due to the far greater range of these missiles, the submarines carrying them would not require 'forward basing' facilities such as Holy Loch. However, in mid-1983 rumours were emerging from Holy Loch that the refit and support facilities there may indeed be kept on beyond the withdrawal of

Poseidon-armed vessels in the early to mid-1990s, and may be used additionally by Trident-armed 'Ohio' class submarines which are due to begin operations with the Atlantic Fleet in the mid-1980s. This disturbing possibility may be implicit in a statement from the US naval attache in London that 'Holy Loch will continue to be needed for valuable basing support until the end of the century.'[75]

Similarly, there are no publicly stated plans to base US navy SSNs at Holy Loch. In view of the current programme of arming these vessels with Tomahawk submarine-launched cruise missiles (SLCMs), many of them with nuclear warheads, from 1983 onwards, any such step would be a serious escalation. There is evidence that SSNs armed with these new weapons will use Holy Loch. In a Dunoon restaurant regularly frequented by US sailors is a small wall plaque. It reads 'Joint Cruise Missiles Project 3'. US SSNs already visit the base periodically, usually for emergency repairs, but these visits are kept quiet. One such vessel, believed to be a 'Skipjack' class, arrived at Holy Loch unexpectedly on 20 December 1982. The refit and maintenance facilities of the *Hunley* are in fact available to virtually any class of submarine. Future use of Holy Loch by both Trident-armed SSBNs and Tomahawk-armed SSNs cannot be ruled out. Without local vigilance it is extremely likely that the USA would attempt to introduce these new weapons to Holy Loch by stealth.

At present the Lafayette and Benjamin Franklin SSBNs come into Holy Loch after each 70 day patrol anywhere in the north-east Atlantic, Norwegian and Barents Seas and Mediterranean, for a 32 day intermediate refit alongside the *Hunley,* and a change of crew. Each SSBN has two crews, known as Blue and Gold. Those entitled to home leave can fly back to the USA on special military charter flights from Prestwick.

If necessary an SSBN can be put into the floating dry dock for repairs or the scraping off of marine growth. The *Hunley* itself (and its sister ship USS *Holland*) was designed specifically to support Poseidon SSBNs. It has '52 separate workshops to provide complete support to nuclear plants, electronic and navigation systems, missiles and other submarine systems.'[76] About 20 Poseidon missiles can be stored inside the *Hunley*. It has been stated that 'during shore preparations, two missiles are rotated each time'[77] which means that the *Hunley*'s crew do not have to lift each SSBN's 16 missiles in and out every 70 days. The missiles themselves are never visible to the public since they are lifted in and out of the submarines by crane inside a special white tube. This allows the US navy to keep the number of missiles actually being moved, and any secret modifications to the missiles, concealed from the prying eyes of Soviet reconnaissance satellites.

Security of the nuclear weapons on board the *Hunley* is provided by a detachment of 45 US marines who are not well-known for their refined behaviour. They are armed with M16 rifles, pump-action shotguns and stun grenades, and stand permanent armed guard behind the heavy steel doors of the nuclear storage area in the aft end of the ship. The doors are marked 'Warning: Deadly Force Is Authorised Beyond This Point'. For those who fail to get the message there is also a large skull and crossbones symbol.

Command of the SSBNs at Holy Loch rests with the US navy's Commander-in-Chief Atlantic (CINCLANT) at Norfolk, Virginia. He exercises control through the Commander-in-Chief US Atlantic Fleet (CINCLANTFLT) and the Commander Submarine Force Atlantic Fleet, as part of the US strategic nuclear forces. Under an agreement established in 1961, 400 of the warheads on the US Poseidon SSBNs (roughly two submarines' worth) are allocated to NATO's Supreme Allied Commander Europe (SACEUR), who would use them as theatre weapons for 'deep interdiction missions against fixed targets.'[78] The *Hunley* maintains communications with its command centres via satellite and other radio links. Through the FLTSATCOM, *Hunley* and the SSBNs may receive orders regarding changes in targeting, patrol areas, etc.

The *Hunley* is clearly a mobile unit capable of autonomous operation. In time of crisis or tension the *Hunley* would move out of Holy Loch, probably to one or several of the West Highland sea lochs which have been equipped with naval mooring buoys since the 1960s. These are Lochs Linnhe, Striven, Long and Fyne. Mobility of this sort has a clear attraction to US plans for protracted nuclear war-fighting capability. Narrow steep-sided lochs may provide some camouflage from satellites, and if *Hunley* was moved around between several locations it would complicate Soviet targeting. The result of this would probably be Soviet warheads landing on every likely mooring site. Exercise deployments of the *Hunley* are designed to practise its war-fighting role. The first of these exercises since *Hunley* replaced *Holland* in early 1982 was due to commence on 8 October 1982, with *Hunley* leaving the Clyde for a two-week 'cruise', with visits to one of five ports: Brest, Liverpool, Portsmouth or an unnamed port in Norway or Portugal. The implications of this for Norway's policy of forbidding nuclear weapons in its territory in peacetime do not seem to have troubled the Americans. The exercise was subsequently postponed until December, then cancelled again, but was likely to be held in 1983. It is noteworthy that during the Cuban missile crisis in 1962 the Polaris mother ship put to sea rather hurriedly, although the Russians may have been relieved to see that it took the crew virtually all night to raise the anchor chains.

Accidents at Holy Loch have been consistently played down by the military. In November 1970 a fire occurred on board the submarine tender while two Polaris SSBNs were moored alongside. In May 1982 fire broke out on one of the tugs moored beside the floating dry dock. There have been innumerable instances of fuel spillage which the base commander does his utmost to conceal from the local population. In early June 1983 the *Hunley* dragged its moorings – a constant worry to the US navy since this could be disastrous while moving missiles. At the same time a badly damaged SSBN was noted alongside the *Hunley*, covered in tarpaulins. It was later shifted to the dry dock. The official line was that it had been damaged when the *Hunley* dragged its moorings, but there have been a number of collisions at sea between US SSBNs and other vessels, including fishing vessels in the Clyde and Irish Sea.

The incident which provoked most public concern occurred in November 1981, when a Poseidon missile being winched between the tender and a submarine ran free. The missile fell 17 feet or, as the US navy put it, 'descended at a faster than normal rate'. Automatic brakes stopped the missile just above the submarine's hull but it swung into the side of the tender. Not only is there evidence that the crane operator handling this missile was either drunk or had been smoking cannabis, but also it is likely that the missile's warheads contained a highly unstable 'trigger' explosive called LX09, whose function is to trigger the chain reaction in the nuclear warhead. LX09 is so dangerous to handle that it is being replaced by a new, supposedly safer material. On this occasion there was fear that the 17ft fall could have triggered the LX09, which would have ignited the missile's rocket fuel and caused a release of radioactive material from the warhead. This would have formed a cloud which would be blown towards Glasgow by the prevailing wind. Although US navy personnel took up station at radiation-protected areas on the tender, no warning was given to the local community or authorities.

Further hazards result from the rubbish produced by the *Hunley* and its submarines. Domestic refuse from the ship is transported across the Clyde to Greenock by puffer for destruction, but children there have come across ampoules of nerve gas antidote and piles of pornographic magazines, while workmen have found open cans of dangerous chemicals and even live ammunition.[79] There is also a regular production of radioactive waste from the submarine reactors.

US fear of activity by the peace movement at Holy Loch is considerable. In congressional hearings in 1979, a representative from Maryland asked a senior USAF General:

> At Holy Loch, anti-nuclear weapons and anti-war groups were mentioned as something of a problem. How closely and at how high a level do we co-operate with British security and intelligence forces?
> *General Brown*: Very closely, including seat of government level. Primary contacts are Special Branch, Scotland Yard, RAF Provost and Security Service, and local constabularies.[80]

When the peace camp was set up in Sandbank early in 1983 and two of its members were arrested for trespassing on the

MOD pier, the US navy called in the MOD police to erect a new fence on the pier and to mount 24 hour patrols around the *Hunley* by motor launch. When asked why this was necessary, one US navy officer on the base stated that while the protests might be peaceful at the moment, 'the PLO started out this way'.[81]

The major concern of the local community in 1982–83 has been the US navy plan to take over the Morris and Lorimer boatyard in Sandbank, double the length of the pier and erect a storage warehouse there. These and other plans are included in the US navy's request for funds for the fiscal year 1984. These consist of a supply pier ($3.26 million), a general warehouse of 25,000 square feet ($3.12 million), a medical/dental clinic in Sandbank ($2.83 million) and a family services centre ($0.6 million).[82] This expansion casts serious doubt on any assurances that the US navy will leave Holy Loch when Poseidon SSBNs are phased out.

146. Inchterf, Kirkintilloch MOD (Procurement Executive) Proof and Experimental Establishment, covering about 180 acres.

Its prime function is determining the quantity of propellant to be used in virtually all the gun and mortar ammunition with which the British services are supplied. It retains the custody of all master standard gun propellants for UK weapons, and monitors their characteristics throughout their service lives and performs a similar function for overseas collaborative projects . . . Inchterf is a closed range, in that all its firings are conducted so that the projectiles are trapped in butts. It also carries out testing of gun and ammunition components such as barrels, breech rings, obturators, cartridge cases, tubes and primers.[83]

There are also detachments of the Materials Quality Assurance Directorate and the RCT railway staff here.

147. Kirk o'Shotts, Lanarkshire Microwave relay station, focal point of several networks. This installation is the link between East Lomond Hill and Sergeant Law in the US navy's UKMS, but this part of the chain may now be disused.

148. Lanark (Winston Barracks)   Army training camp and area.

149. Loch Fyne   Admiralty Marine Technology Establishment (AMTE) underwater noise range 'primarily for routine measurement of noise emitted by naval vessels and submarines, but . . . also used for other acoustic purposes.'[84] On the south shore of Loch Fyne, near St Margarets, is a shore facility which is believed to be the control centre for the passive sonar arrays under the loch. Vickers Oceanic are also active in Loch Fyne conducting underwater trials work which is probably military-related. Loch Fyne is ideal for testing underwater noise emission since it is very deep and has little other traffic on it. The AMTE range is used not only by British submarines but a wide range of NATO vessels. The Dutch submarine *Tijgerhaai*, believed to be one of those based at Faslane, was noted on the surface off Inveraray in early December 1982. 'Oberon' class diesel patrol submarines are also regular users of the range. One of the primary peacetime roles of these types of submarine is covert surveillance (similar to the Soviet w-137 which became rather 'overt' on the rocks off Sweden in 1981). The Loch Fyne range is probably used to perfect techniques of silent underwater operations.

The Admiralty mooring buoys further down Loch Fyne, south of Ardrishaig, may be connected with the AMTE range, or could be earmarked as a wartime dispersal mooring for the US navy SSBN mother ship from the Holy Loch.

150. Lochgilphead (Blairbuie), Argyll   TAVR small-arms range.

151. Loch Striven, Argyll   A large square area of seabed off Brackley Point is used for naval trials, with an undersea cable link to the east shore of the loch at Brackley Point. This is believed to be another AMTE noise range.

152. Loch Striven, Argyll   NATO POL depot built 1960-63 at a cost of £3 million, with NATO Infrastructure Programme funds. Used for refuelling of a wide range of NATO surface ships and diesel-powered submarines. The oil storage tanks cover around 100 acres.

153. Lowther Hill, Dumfries-shire   Primary and secondary surveillance radar station, providing air traffic control over most of central and southern Scotland. Radar data from here is fed to SCATCC Prestwick by BT microwave radio. This would be a vital installation for controlling the flow of the US air armada into Europe during crisis or wartime.

154. Machrihanish, Kintyre RAF airfield with the longest runway in Scotland (10,000 feet), functioning primarily as a wartime and exercise forward operating base for NATO long-range maritime patrol aircraft (LRMPAS).

Machrihanish was originally built for the Fleet Air Arm in 1940. Between 1960 and 1962 NATO funds were used to build the vast new runway, hangars, fuel storage, US navy and RAF weapons stores and accommodation. The original cost of £1.5 million had escalated to over £3 million by the time 18 (Maritime) Group RAF took command of the airfield in May 1963. A further £11 million expansion from 1979 has included runway resurfacing and new airfield lighting (£3 million, completed July 1981), new fuel storage and pipelines for a fast-feeder fuel system (in progress 1982) and new mess facilities (construction to commence 1984). A spokesman at RAF Pitreavie said of these developments, 'it is not on the cards that it will become a nuclear base'.[89] This is because it already is one. The US navy has a store here for Mk.101 and B-57 nuclear depth bombs for use by US navy and NATO LRMPAS. Further expansion has occurred since, with the arrival of a US Naval Special Warfare Unit and RAF police training.

Nuclear depth bombs

The introduction of the Marconi Stingray torpedo to the RAF in 1982 prompted comments in the aviation press that the RAF would henceforth be able to reduce its reliance on the US-supplied and controlled nuclear depth bomb (NDB) 'which is at present a standard weapon with the Nimrod force'.[85] There are some doubts that Stingray can in fact perform such a role, and in this case the willingness of NATO to use nuclear weapons at sea is clear. This has important implications for NATO strategy. There have been suggestions that nuclear war might be initiated at sea with the use of tactical nuclear weapons by ships, submarines or aircraft. The military have positively encouraged the belief that these weapons can be used at sea without escalation, although that is not official policy.[86]

It has been stated that a submarine with a hull capable of diving to 2,000 feet would be destroyed by a 10 kiloton nuclear weapon exploding within about 1½ miles when the submarine is at a depth of 500 feet. If a submarine is known to be at around 500 feet and somewhere within an area of 50 square miles then 12 such weapons would ensure its destruction.[87] Weapons such as Subroc and Asroc, carried by submarines and ships respectively, were said to be for use against fast, deep-diving nuclear submarines even though when they were first deployed (about 1962) the USSR did not have such submarines. The real reason for their deployment was, at least initially, that the 'overkill' provided by using a nuclear weapon would more than compensate for the relatively poor submarine target location possible at that time. When NDBS were introduced the military expected to engage in a short nuclear war rather than the 'protracted' conflict they now anticipate.

Modern homing torpedoes with programmable sensors have a very high probability of hitting their target first and may enable attacks against Soviet submarines without recourse to nuclear anti-submarine weapons. However, the deployment of nuclear anti-submarine weapons is likely to continue as they are unaffected by possible Soviet counter-measures against NATO homing torpedoes, or other factors such as stronger hulls. The USA is pressing ahead with development of the ASW Stand-Off Weapon to replace Subroc, and a recent US Senate Subcommittee study concluded that the US navy should continue with nuclear weapons already deployed and extend the role of nuclear weapons into other areas.[88]

The units and personnel based at Machrihanish are as follows:

(a) 300 RAF personnel, chiefly associated with handling and maintenance of air-dropped anti-submarine weapons – the US Mk.46 and British Stingray torpedoes. These can regularly be seen on lorries between Machrihanish and Glasgow.

(b) Approximately 20 US navy personnel of the Naval Aviation Weapons Facility Detachment, responsible for maintenance, storage, handling and security of Mk.101 and/or B-57 nuclear depth bombs for use by the US navy P-3 Orions, RAF Nimrods and German and Dutch Atlantics which are assigned to Machrihanish in wartime. These weapons are operated under the dual key 'permissive action link' system in which US navy personnel have ultimate responsibility for arming the weapons before they are used by another NATO member. Until 1982 the Dutch navy's Neptune aircraft were also assigned to use NDBS stored at Machrihanish. Neptunes have now been replaced by Orions, and although these have not yet been equipped for the nuclear role the Dutch parliament was due to decide in 1983 on 'the possible transfer of the Neptune's capability in carrying nuclear depth charges.'[90] The NDBS at Machrihanish are periodically 'rotated' to the USA for overhaul. It is believed that they are transported in USAF C-5 Galaxy aircraft on 'special cargo' flights.

(c) Approximately 20 personnel of the US Naval Mobile Mine Assembly Group, Detachment Two, whose job is to maintain, assemble, store and issue underwater mines for use by NATO. The reference to 'Mobile' in the title may refer to the mines or to the unit itself. If the former, then this unit is probably concerned with the Submarine-Launched Mobile Mine (SLMM), which

> is intended to provide the American fleet with a capability for planting mines in shallow water (to approximately 100 metres) by submarine, using a self-propelled mine to reach water inaccessible to other vehicles. It is also meant for use in locations where covert mining would be particularly desirable from a tactical standpoint.[91]

In short, they would be used by US submarines operating very close to Soviet military ports in areas such as the Kola Peninsula.

It is not clear why such a unit should be assembling mines for use by NATO. The SLMM is only in service with the US navy, and there would seem to be no reason for conventional mines for non-US forces to be held in US custody.

Conventional ammunition is also held by the US navy at Machrihanish. A stock-taking of these weapons was completed in 1982.

(d) US Naval Special Warfare Unit 2 (NSWU 2). This is a special forces unit, the US navy equivalent of the British Special

Boat Squadron (SBS), but with more of an offensive role on land than the latter. According to official statements, NSWU 2 is a NATO-assigned unit, probably under the command of SACLANT to operate fifth column spying and sabotage missions behind Soviet lines on the Northern Flank. US Naval Special Warfare troops are known as 'SEALS' (SEa–Air–Land). The unit moved into Machrihanish in March 1981 with a core of 17 permanently-based personnel and six-month training detachments of about 20 other SEALS from the USA. Training in clandestine operations, particularly 'infiltration and exfiltration', is conducted locally, with parachute drops on land and sea, diving exercises and operations from a 36 ft Seafox light special warfare craft which is sometimes moored at an MOD-reserved section of the Old Quay in Campbeltown. NSWU 2 holds regular exercises with its SAS and SBS counterparts. In wartime it would form, with other special forces units, part of the 'Special Operations Task Force Europe', creating disruption and confusion behind enemy lines. There is some evidence that US special forces also carry out these activities in peacetime – certainly in South-east Asia and Central America – and the proximity of Northern Ireland to Machrihanish suggests that joint SAS/SBS/NSWU exercises here may be used to exchange tactics and methods.

Like most special forces units, NSWU 2 has been the subject of a media/military smokescreen over its activities. In March 1983 journalists on *The Guardian* and the *Daily Mail* were told by an unnamed military source that NSWU 2 had only just moved into Machrihanish, and that its role was to combat piracy in the Irish Sea and to operate sonar equipment for detection of Soviet submarines and ships. Neither of these bears any resemblance to the true function of US navy special forces, which are currently being given 'a more prominent role in the Pentagon's military planning'[92] to intervene in any crisis or conflict anywhere in the world.

(e) RAF Police School detachment. This unit moved into Machrihanish in 1982 from its main base at Newton, Nottinghamshire. About 30 personnel here conduct the final phase of the RAF police training programme – primarily rock climbing and survival training in the areas around Bordadubh, Loch Lussa and the Mull of Kintyre.

Machrihanish's wartime role as a base for NATO LRMPAS operating in anti-submarine and anti-shipping roles in the eastern Atlantic is practised regularly in the annual NATO autumn exercises and in Joint Maritime Course (JMC) exercises. The base is used by RAF Nimrods from Kinloss, US navy Orions detached from Keflavik or US bases, Canadian Auroras, German, Dutch and, less frequently, French Atlantics, and, from 1984, the new Dutch Orions. The British, American, Dutch and possibly German aircraft would use the Mk.101 and B-57 NDBS stored here. Stocks of spare parts for wartime-assigned LRMPAS are also held here. From 1984 'RAF Machrihanish will be the first location for a secondary spares supply' for Dutch navy Orions.[93]

In the apparent absence of nuclear weapons stores at Prestwick and Kinloss it seems that the nuclear-capable RN Sea Kings and RAF Nimrods at these respective bases would fly to Machrihanish to pick up their NDBS. Certainly Kinloss Nimrods and Prestwick-based Sea Kings are the most regular users of this base. This would mean that British-made and British-controlled NDBS (as used on the Sea King) are also present at Machrihanish, though there is currently no evidence for this.

With no permanently-based aircraft, and being in an isolated area, Machrihanish attracts an extremely diverse range of military exercises. Since 1975 it has been used for exercises by US navy RH-53D mine counter-measures helicopters, TAVR and SAS troops, a USMC/RMC amphibious assault on Arran, simulated wartime combat aircrew rescue exercises, low-flying by German and RAF transports, an international oceanographic research project off Rockall, US army Chinook helicopter heavy-lift operations, and as a temporary base for RAF Nimrods from Kinloss and RAF Phantoms from Leuchars.

In 1978 Machrihanish was considered (but rejected on cost grounds) as a base for USAF KC-135 tanker aircraft. It may still be earmarked for this role, since it lies under the eastern end of one of the main air refuelling areas used by USAF and US navy aircraft deploying to Europe. The fast-feeder fuel system built in 1981–82 would be ideally suited to operations by combat aircraft too, and it is no coincidence that Machrihanish has been suggested as one of the west coast forward operating bases for the RAF's new Tornado F.2 interceptors.[94] Other possible roles for Machrihanish concern US reinforcement of Europe. With a long runway and considerable support facilities it would be a key transit point for transport and combat planes en route to Europe. It may also be used in future by detachments of US Marine Corps combat aircraft assigned to the Northern Flank.

Machrihanish's nuclear facilities, diversity of based units and grossly under-utilised capabilities make it one of the most important bases to watch for military expansion.

155. Moorland, Eskdalemuir Originally a UKAEA seismic monitoring post for underground nuclear tests, but now a NERC geomagnetic and seismological observatory. Similar stations in Norway, New Zealand and elsewhere are known to be linked in real time to the US National Security Agency so that, for example, spy satellites can be moved into orbits suitable for investigating possible Soviet or Chinese nuclear tests indicated by the sensors. This data might also assist in conducting a nuclear war by indicating whether US warheads were accurately hitting their targets.

156. Portavadie, Loch Fyne This government-built oil platform construction yard, which never received an order, was surveyed in 1981 by both the RN and the US navy as a possible wartime or emergency naval base. In 1982 the Scottish Office decided to fill in the site and demolish the buildings, but 'the jetty and approach road would be retained and . . . might in the longer term be capable of further development', [95] so naval interest may literally resurface.

157. Port Glasgow TAVR centre with infantry and RCT units, also A Squadron, 23 SAS Regiment TAVR.

158. Powfoot, Annan Explosives factory operated by Nobel Explosive Co. Ltd (an ICI subsidiary) as agents for the MOD. In 1973 it consisted of an explosives plant and a propellant plant, providing a total of 100 jobs. It is not clear whether the former is still in operation, but in 1981 Powfoot was described as 'the only UK source of single base propellants. The main products are rifle and cannon powders.'[96] Nugent reported in 1973 that local farmers complained of damage to their property and competition for local labour from the factory, and wanted it closed.[97]

159. Prestwick, Ayrshire British Airports Authority (BAA) airport with declining civil use (mainly transatlantic flights) but important military status:

(a) Royal Navy HMS *Gannet*, base of seven Sea King anti-submarine helicopters and 263 RN personnel of 819 Squadron. Its tasks are anti-submarine protection of the Clyde SSBN bases, exercises with submarines and surface ships, rapid transport of Commachio Company marines to offshore oil rigs, anti-gun running patrols off Northern Ireland and a Department of Trade contract for search and rescue provision in the west of Scotland.

Sea Kings can carry up to four Mk.46 or Stingray torpedoes or British-built nuclear depth bombs. These may be stored at Machrihanish for use by 819 Squadron.

The unit is accommodated in buildings vacated by the USAF in 1966 and modernised in 1981 at a cost of £1.5 million. Rumours surfaced in 1983 that the RN is about to base a second Sea King squadron at Prestwick.

(b) RAF Prestwick, Atlantic House. This is the military section of the Scottish Air Traffic Control Centre, known as SCATCC(Mil). It receives data from air traffic control radars all round Scotland and controls military aircraft via the NATS UHF radio relay network. Atlantic House also contains the Oceanic Control Centre, which controls all air traffic over the North Atlantic and would be a vital element in the US reinforcement of Europe. Also here are an Air Defence Notification Centre, believed to be responsible for collation of data from NATS radars in Scotland for onward transmission to the Air Defence Data Centre at West Drayton, and a Distress and Diversion Cell which receives transmissions from military aircraft in distress through the MOD Auto-Triangulation Service receivers at Stornoway, Tiree, Wick and elsewhere.

(c) The USAF Military Airlift Command (MAC) had a main

base at Prestwick until 1966 to support transatlantic flights by US military cargo, personnel and combat aircraft. In-flight refuelling and longer-range aircraft reduced the need for this base, but with a 9,800ft runway and very little civil traffic Prestwick remains one of the prime designated airfields in the UK for receipt of US reinforcements. MAC C-141s operate 15 cargo flights a month here in support of US bases in Scotland, and there are also two personnel flights a week by US airliners under military contract. A large proportion of these are for SSBN crews returning to the USA for home leave from Holy Loch. The USAF has five enlisted personnel at Prestwick to handle these flights.

Early in 1983 it was revealed in the USAF's budget request for 1984 that a major expansion was proposed for Prestwick.[98] This consisted of a 20,000 square foot, $1.83 million forward storage warehouse for combat aircraft spares for USAF units in Europe. This was part of the European Distribution System, designed to wartime standards to speed the flow of spare parts to combat units and thereby greatly increase the number of combat sorties the USAF could launch in wartime. Shortly after this announcement was made, the USAF stated that, having inspected the potential facilities at Prestwick, they had decided not to go ahead. In the meantime considerable anger had been generated by the fact that neither the MOD, the local authorities nor the local MP had been consulted about the USAF plan.

Although the European Distribution System plan was dropped, Prestwick is ripe for US military expansion. Likely developments are a major transportation terminal for US military reinforcements, US Marine Corps facilities or forward operating base facilities for US-based combat planes.

(d) British Aerospace Scottish Division has a factory at Prestwick with 1,820 employees which has done a considerable amount of military work (building Bulldog and Jetstream trainers and sections of Hercules transports, and repair of Canadian Starfighters based in Germany).

160. Prestwick (Monkswell House), Ayrshire The HQ 25 Group ROC, controlling some 40 nuclear blast and fall-out monitoring posts in south-west Scotland.

161. Rhu, Helensburgh

(a) Royal Corps of Transport Port Unit, from which one of the army's two Landing Craft Logistic (LCLS) operates supply services to South Uist and St Kilda in support of the Hebrides Missile Range. A new storage building and jetty were built in 1980–81.

(b) An RN monitoring station. This controls ship and submarine movements in and out of Faslane, and is believed to control, in conjunction with the RNR HQ Unit at Greenock, the anti-submarine sonar system in the Clyde. The installation was extended in 1981.

162. Rhu Staffnish, Kintyre NATS VHF/UHF radio relay for communication with civil and military aircraft for air traffic control.

163. Rosneath, Gare Loch

(a) NATO Oil Fuel Depot, on 33 acres of MOD land, operated by BP under an international agreement with NATO users. Built 1960-62 at a cost of £250,000. Mostly used by vessels associated with Faslane.

(b) Stroul Bay: RN degaussing ranges, for de-magnetising the hulls and equipment of naval vessels to stop them setting off magnet mines.

164. Sergeant Law, Barrhead Microwave relay station in the US navy UKMS chain. Believed to have been disused since the US navy closed its radio station in Northern Ireland in 1978, but equipment still in place and could be reactivated.

165. Skipness, Kintyre MOD calibration range, established 1976–77. Believed to operate with vessels on trials in the Clyde.

166. Stranraer TAVR Royal Military Police, a detachment of 243 Provost Company.

167. Toward, Dunoon MOD radio transmitter, established 1978–79. Believed to be for short range naval communications.

168. Troon, Ayrshire Vehicles of 251 Fuel Tanker Squadron RCT(V).

169. West Freugh, Stranraer Royal Aircraft Establishment (RAE) outstation, consisting of a 2,750 acre airfield and 21 smaller sites connected with a number of trials ranges. Danger areas for the ranges associated with West Freugh cover most of

Loch Ryan and Luce Bay and a further 250 square miles off the west coast of Galloway.

West Freugh is run by the Ranges Division of the RAE's Instrumentation and Trials Department. It is 'dedicated to trials involving high-speed, low-level air attack.'[99] For this purpose there are a number of targets on the shores of Luce Bay and moored in the bay. Weapons tested at West Freugh in the last few years include the Martel and Blowpipe missiles, cluster bombs, the JP233 runway-cratering bomb, laser-guided bombs and their associated navigation/attack equipment. In 1961 the ranges were used for test drops of the Skybolt strategic nuclear missile.

Also in Luce Bay is a Sonar Drop Test Range, where research and development is conducted on new air-dropped sonobuoys and the Electrical Quality Assurance Directorate tests samples from each production batch of sonobuoys for the RAF and RN.

The West Freugh/Luce Bay ranges are also used by RAF and other NATO strike/attack aircraft for training.

The RAE has its own fleet of three Buccaneer and one Andover aircraft, and several small vessels, to support work on the ranges.

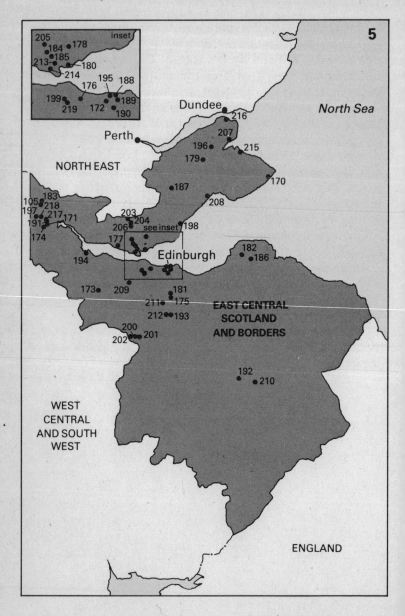

Section five: East Central Scotland and Borders

170. Anstruther (Troy Wood), Fife Ex-RAF radar station which now serves as the bunker for Northern Zone Control, from where around 200 Scottish Office, police and military personnel will attempt to govern most of Scotland north of the central lowlands in wartime.

171. Bandeath, Stirling An RN armament depot, serving Rosyth.

172. Barnton Quarry, Edinburgh Scottish Central Control wartime bunker, maintained by Division 1c of the SHHD. It would house the Secretary of State for Scotland and up to 300 personnel from the Scottish Office, police, BBC, BT and other organisations, exercising overall control of wartime government in Scotland.

Following post-war use by the Royal Auxiliary Air Force, this bunker was identified by the 'Spies for Peace' in 1963 as one of Britain's Regional Seats of Government. It was modernised for its current role in the late 1960s. The bunker extends right underneath Corstorphine Hill, apparently emerging in one place near the lion's den at Edinburgh Zoo in the shape of an empty green telephone box.

In 1974, to the great embarrassment of the authorities, four youths broke into the bunker and stole £2,000 worth of radio gear.

173. Bathgate, West Lothian TAVR infantry, a detachment of A Company, 1st Battalion 52nd Lowland Volunteers.

174. Cambusbarron, Stirling Army training area used by local infantry and TAVR units.

175. Castlelaw Hill, Midlothian Army firing range, established in 1935, covering 965 acres, with an 18-target range used only at night by regular, TAVR and cadet units in the Edinburgh area. In 1969 British army involvement in Northern Ireland led to increased firing range requirements. The MOD informed the local authorities that they intended to build a 120 firer electric target range at Castlelaw by 1973-74 to meet this need. Considerable opposition from planners, conservationists and those interested in the outdoor recreation value of the Pentland Hills led to a public inquiry in 1979. During the inquiry the Principal Staff Officer of the army in Scotland claimed that 'large numbers of people will walk by the area who will be oblivious of the noise because of the clatter of their prams and the barking of their dogs.'[100] Up to 11,000 rifle and machine gun rounds will be fired each day on the range.

The reporter to the inquiry recommended that the range should go to an alternative site 'subject to overriding national considerations'. As with the Stornoway inquiry in 1981, this left the way open to the Secretary of State to give the go-ahead despite the recommendations made to him. The new range is due for completion in late 1983 at a cost of over £2 million.

176. Craigiehall, Edinburgh HQ Army, Scotland. This administrative, command and control installation would have a central role in Scotland's wartime government. The General Staff Branch at Craigiehall has responsiblility for four main areas of army activity in Scotland: operations and staff duties; home defence plans; security and mobilisation; and training. Representatives of all the major corps in the army are here, and there are a number of specialist units responsible for the HQ's functioning in peace and war. These include a security unit from the Intelligence Corps, the main bomb disposal unit for Scotland, a Royal Military Police Special Investigation Branch unit (the Army's CID) and a Royal Corps of Transport unit which provides the staff cars and other transport needs of the HQ.

Of most interest, however, are the communications functions of Craigiehall, which are focused in a communications centre run largely by WRACS belonging to 242 Signals Squadron. This unit operates a variety of systems including standard BT landlines, the military's BOXER microwave system (both of which carry the day-to-day message traffic between HQS and other units) and, in the near future, the new wartime command network known as MOULD. This is a network of automatic VHF/UHF remote repeater stations on hilltops around the UK. Construction started in the London area in 1982; when complete it will be one of the main systems used in the wartime military government of the UK. Craigiehall may also be linked into wider UK and NATO systems such as the DCN and TASS.

177. Crombie, Fife The main RN armament depot for Rosyth. It also supplies unspecified equipment to about 90 army and marines units in Scotland.

178. Cullaloe Hill, Fife This hilltop site for a microwave relay station was acquired by the MOD in 1981, and is destined to become one of the key military communications nodes in Scotland, linking a number of telecommunications systems including BOXER, UKADGE and the BT network, as part of the development of the NATO Integrated Communications System (NICS). Cullaloe will link the command centres at Pitreavie and Craigiehall to the new NATO satellite communications terminal at Balado Bridge, with links into the BT microwave network via East Lomond Hill in Fife and Blackcastle Hill in East Lothian. This will allow exchanges of data between such NATO networks as TARE and TASS on the one hand, and UKADGE, NADGE, BOXER, and possibly the US navy's UK Microwave System on the other. 'Project UNITER' is also believed to be connected with the development of the Cullaloe site. UNITER is a new digital RAF ground communications system in the UK which, when complete in the mid-1990s, will provide 'a secure, survivable and integrated network.'[101]

The Cullaloe project is being undertaken by the NICS Management Agency, and has been at the planning stages for a number of years. It is thought that problems with NATO funding have delayed its implementation. Until it is built the new satellite terminal at Balado Bridge is unlikely to become fully operational.

179. Cupar, Fife TAVR centre, vehicles of 239 Squadron, RCT(V).

180. Donibristle, Fife Defence Lands Office, Scotland, of the Department of the Environment's Property Services Agency. This looks after all military land, buildings and construction projects in Scotland.

181. Dreghorn, Edinburgh Army camp, training area and firing range of 889 acres, in use since 1913. Three small-arms ranges with 24 targets and a grenade range are used in daylight only, primarily by infantry units from Ritchie Camp, Redford Barracks and Glencorse, and TAVR units. When the new firing range at Castlelaw is opened the Dreghorn ranges will close, but the land will be retained by the MOD for use as a training area for, amongst other things, Scorpion and Scimitar light tanks, armoured cars and other vehicles and helicopters. Strong pressure from the local authorities and others to close Dreghorn and establish a Pentlands Country Park have met solid resistance from the MOD.

182. Drem, East Lothian SHHD civil defence material testing station and bridge depot, with emergency bailey bridges for use in wartime.

183. Dunblane, Stirling

    (a) Vehicles of D Troop, 231 Squadron, RCT(V); and

    (b) Queen Victoria School, for army children.

184. Dunfermline, Fife TAVR centre, HQ of 153 (Highland) Transport Regiment and 231 Squadron, both RCT(V).

185. Dunfermline (St Leonard's Hill), Fife Admiralty Marine Technology Establishment (AMTE) Structures Department, which conducts research into the welding of ship and submarine hulls, the vulnerability of ships and submarines to explosives, noise and vibration reduction, submarine pressure hull design and surface ship structures. Considerable use is made of dock and test facilities at Rosyth and trials ranges in the Firth of Forth.

186. East Fortune, East Lothian SHHD civil defence store for 'fire-fighting equipment, gas masks, sand bags and probably supplies of CS and CR anti-riot gas.'[102] Ironically East Fortune also houses the Scottish Fire Service Training School, and the Fire Brigades Union has a long-standing policy of not co-operating in civil defence exercises.

187. East Lomond Hill, Fife Microwave relay station in both the BT and US navy networks. All stations south of Kinnaber in the latter chain apparently closed in 1978, but East Lomond is one of the planned interchange points between the 'civil' BT system and the NATO Integrated Communications System, via Cullaloe Hill.

188. Edinburgh A number of military installations are spread round the city. TAVR units include three Air Defence troops (with Blowpipe missiles), two infantry companies, a company of Paras, an Engineer Squadron, two RCT squadrons, an RMP Provost Company, a signals squadron and the HQ of 23 Security Company, Intelligence and Security Group (v). There are also naval, air force and army reserve units connected with the universities, and the Royal Auxiliary Air Force's No.2 (City of Edinburgh) Maritime Headquarters Unit also has a base in the town. Its personnel

> monitor the movements of potentially hostile surface and below-surface vessels in peacetime, and co-operate with Nimrod long-range maritime reconnaissance and anti-submarine aircraft of No.18 Group to keep this country's vital sealanes clear of enemy interference in wartime. The men and women volunteers receive a thorough training in communications, in the operation and control of RAF aircraft far out over the oceans, and in the guidance of ships of the Royal Navy into attack positions.[103]

This work is conducted at the Maritime HQ at Pitreavie, supporting regular RN and RAF operations staff.

MOD(PE) also has personnel in Edinburgh, with the Electrical Quality Assurance Directorate and the CSDE Project Team at Ferranti's and the Naval Ship Production Overseer for Scotland. The RAMC has a medical reception station in the south side of the city.

189. Edinburgh Castle   The HQ 52 Lowland Brigade, which controls all Scottish army units south of a line from Fife Ness to the Mull of Kintyre; HQ the Scottish Division, administering infantry recruitment and training in Scotland; Regimental HQ of several Scottish infantry regiments; and base of a Provost Company of the Royal Military Police which is assigned to home defence and would be responsible for controlling troop movements and traffic on Scotland's essential service routes in wartime.

190. Edinburgh (Redford Barracks)   Normally houses at least one infantry battalion. Support facilities include a detachment of 26 Command Workshop, REME.

191. Forthside, Stirling   Army ordnance depot, modernised in the late 1970s with a new 11,000 square metre storage building.

Also the base of 26 Command Workshop, REME, which repairs and maintains the vehicles and equipment of virtually all army units in Scotland. Forthside also has a detachment of RCT railway staff, who not only operate the depot's internal railway sidings but 'would take over some civilian railways in an emergency.'[104]

192. Galashiels, Borders TAVR infantry, one and a half companies of 52nd Lowland Volunteers.

193. Glencorse, Midlothian Scottish infantry depot, which trains up to 1,500 recruits a year for all the Scottish infantry regiments.

194. Grangemouth, West Lothian

(a) An important wartime military port which has a 'normally unmanned US army and navy transportation terminal'[105] for movement of US reinforcements to Europe.

(b) TAVR units in the town are one troop of 131 Independent Parachute Squadron, RE(v); a troop of 225 Squadron, RCT(v); C Company, 3rd Battalion 51st Highland Volunteers, and the Shell-sponsored 502 Specialist Team, RE(v) (Bulk Petroleum), most of whose members work at Shell's Grangemouth plant. The unit's wartime task would be repair and maintenance of fuel pipelines and storage tanks.

195. Granton, Edinburgh HMS *Claverhouse* (RNR Sea Training Centre) and HMS *Forth* (Forth Division, RNR) training on inshore minesweepers.

196. Hawklaw, Cupar, Fife Composite Signals Organisation Station, part of the GCHQ SIGINT network. Hawklaw has been a communications eavesdropping installation since the Second World War. Its special assignment is to listen in to 'commercial traffic – private, international telegrams and telex messages, known in the trade as International Licence Carrier communications.'[106] This probably includes the communications of neutral countries such as Sweden and Finland and Britain's NATO allies as well as the Warsaw Pact countries. The equipment at Hawklaw produces hard copies of messages on teletype. These are then retransmitted to GCHQ at Cheltenham for further analysis.

Government Communications Headquarters (GCHQ)

GCHQ is not a single location but is the cover name given to the British state signals intelligence gathering agency. This engages in the 'reception and analysis of foreign communications and other electronic transmissions for intelligence purposes.'[107]

Officially, GCHQ is the Signals Department of the Foreign Office but recent investigations and spy trials show that its remit is even wider than the above quote suggests. It provides the bulk of Britain's foreign intelligence – economic, diplomatic, political and military. With an annual budget estimated at £200 million and some 20,000 personnel, it is a sinister and unaccountable organisation.

Journalists have revealed widespread corruption at its listening bases worldwide and have shown that GCHQ hides behind the curtain of 'national security' and the Official Secrets Act, with backing at the highest level, to cover up its corruption, gross inefficiency, extravagance and lax security.[108]

GCHQ is a senior partner, covering Africa and Europe west of the Urals, in the once secret UKUSA SIGINT Pact, headed by the US National Security Agency (NSA). While GCHQ conducts the 'respectable' business of monitoring its perceived enemies, the Warsaw Pact, it also breaches international laws and conventions by listening in to NATO allies, EEC members, foreign dissidents (under 'Project Minaret') and neutral countries. Intercepted material is passed on to the NSA. Similarly the NSA illegally intercepts British government communications (as part of Project 'Wideband Extraction') and international private and commercial communications, from its bases in the UK (see Craigowl Hill). It is likely that the NSA is logging data on potential 'troublemakers' (trade unionists, peace activists, etc.) who might cause problems for the USA as it sought to establish *de facto* control of the UK during the run up to a 'limited' nuclear war in Europe.

Since 1963 GCHQ's non-military signals monitoring has been done by its civilian front agency, the Composite Signals Organisation (CSO), which has two listening stations in Scotland at Brora and Hawklaw.[109]

197. Hayford Mill, Stirling SHHD civil defence equipment store.

198. Kirkcaldy, Fife TAVR centre, B Company, 51st Highland Volunteers and a troop of vehicles of 239 Squadron, RCT(V).

199. Kirkliston, West Lothian RN Royal Elizabeth Yard, a supply and stores depot for Rosyth.

200. Kirknewton Airfield, Midlothian MOD(Air) airfield, currently used only by Air Cadets gliders and occasional visits by Army Air Corps aircraft in connection with nearby Ritchie Camp. Army parachute training is also carried out here. This base was a USAF SIGINT station until 1966, tapping international commercial radio communications.

201. Kirknewton, Midlothian SHHD Eastern Zone Control bunker, responsible for the wartime government of Lothian and Borders Regions. Two buildings – a 1950s war room and a concrete blockhouse – were joined together and modernised for the current role around 1972.

202. Kirknewton (Ritchie Camp), Midlothian Army camp, housing one infantry battalion.

203. Knock Hill, Dunfermline, Fife An RN radio station, believed to be associated with Pitreavie. This installation may have engaged in early trials of the MATELO system (see *Milltown*), and it is a likely location for recent trials conducted by the Admiralty Surface Weapons Establishment (ASWE) Communications Division in the propagation of HF radio signals to exploit digital signal processing techniques and devices. For this purpose 'ASWE has a small outstation in Scotland which is used for carrying out propagation trials.'[110]

204. Knockhill, Dunfermline, Fife An RN rifle range used by personnel from Rosyth.

205. Lathalmond, Fife An RN store depot, serving Rosyth.

206. Lethans Muir, Dunfermline, Fife An RAF HF radio station, believed to have been closed and sold to the Forestry Commission in 1981.

207. Leuchars, Fife The UK's prime air defence airfield, base of 35 RAF Phantom FG.1 interceptors. The two resident squadrons, 43 and 111, share the task of 'Northern QRA' (Quick Reaction Alert) in peacetime. The HQ 11 Group RAF at Bentley Priory in Middlesex allocates aircraft at Leuchars (or other fighter bases) the task of intercepting any unidentified radar contacts approaching UK airspace – usually many hundreds of miles north of Shetland.

The British public is constantly fed the notion that these interceptions are a daily occurrence, with RAF fighter pilots continually airborne to fend off naked Soviet aggression round our shores. This is a fallacy. The number of interceptions of Soviet aircraft off UK airspace has, on the RAF's own figures, declined from a peak of up to six per week in 1980 to only four a week in 1982. On average three of these involve Phantoms from Leuchars.[111] Virtually all of the intercepted Soviet aircraft are Bear and Badger maritime reconnaissance aircraft, not 'bombers', and the notion that RAF fighters have to frantically scramble into the air to catch them before they reach the British coast is also extremely misleading. In fact, they are tracked all the way down the Norwegian Sea by NADGE and other radars in Norway, Faeroes and Iceland. The scramble order is passed to Leuchars in time for a Phantom to reach its Combat Air Patrol (CAP) point over the Atlantic just before the Bear or Badger approaches the area. This is designed to save RAF fighters from needlessly burning up fuel and aircrew hours over the Iceland–Faeroes gap.

The wartime role of 43 Squadron is not the air defence of Britain but air defence of the fleet in the north-east Atlantic and US reinforcements crossing to Europe. It is assigned to SAC-LANT, and would be a major user of an expanded NATO base at Stornoway. No. 111 Squadron is assigned in both peace and war to SACEUR as one of the five squadrons defending UK airspace. The Phantoms in both squadrons will be replaced by Tornado F.2s from around 1986–87.

Early in 1983 construction work started on a massive 'hardening' programme at Leuchars, designed to make the base capable of continued operations in a prolonged conventional war. The first phase of this work involves the erection of 22 hardened aircraft shelters, squadron HQ buildings, offices, personnel and fuel bowser buildings and underground fuel storage. Balfour Beatty holds this £20 million NATO-funded contract, which is due for completion in 1985. The hardened aircraft shelters are designed to withstand a direct hit from a 500lb bomb or a near miss from a 1,000lb bomb. They are also sealed against fall-out and chemical and biological weapons, and could withstand the blast effects of a nuclear explosion several miles away. Other major construction works at Leuchars will bring the total to £50 million.

A further element in the drive to make Leuchars more 'survivable' and therefore to guarantee its war-fighting capability is the formation in March 1983 of 277 (Airfield Damage Repair) Field Squadron, RE(v). This unit's 82 members are trained to repair bomb damage to the airfield's runway as rapidly as possible in order to continue operating in war. This is the first of eight such TAVR units to be established at RAF airfields in the UK.

Leuchars is a 'Master Diversionary Airfield', open 24 hours a day, and receives regular visits and training detachments of RAF and other NATO strike/attack and air defence aircraft. However despite this use, and suggestions in some CND publications, there is no nuclear weapons store at Leuchars. The only armaments stored here are Skyflash, Sparrow and Sidewinder air-to-air and Rapier surface-to-air missiles, and SUU-23 cannon.

Anti-aircraft defence of the airfield is provided by the Rapier missiles of 27 Squadron RAF Regiment, which in late 1982 was the only Rapier unit in the UK equipped with Marconi Blindfire radar, which gives the system a night/bad weather capability. This unit has a major role in promoting British arms sales overseas. It 'demonstrates the weapon system to many potential overseas customers. During 1981 the unit hosted visits from delegations representing the USA (four times), Ecuador (twice), Norway and Singapore.'[112]

Leuchars also houses two Wessex rescue helicopters, the Scottish detachment of the RAF Provost and Security Services (responsible for internal security and counter-intelligence) and a detachment of ROC personnel from Caledonian Sector Control, Craigiebarns, who form a Nuclear Reporting Cell to provide advice to the RAF on dispersal of the base's aircraft to 'safe' or 'clean' areas during a nuclear war.

208. Leven, Fife TAVR centre, one troop of 239 Squadron RCT(v) and a detachment of 243 Provost Company, RMP(v).

209. Livingston Station, West Lothian Royal Engineers depot, known as 324 Engineer Park. This unit is thought to comprise the vehicles, personnel and equipment which would be assigned to home defence engineering tasks in Scotland in wartime – road and bridge repair, water supply maintenance, rubble clearance, etc.

210. Melrose, Borders TAVR small-arms range.

211. Milton Bridge, Midlothian Army training area, used largely by recruits from the Glencorse infantry depot.

212. Penicuik, Midlothian TAVR infantry, 1st Company, 2nd Battalion 52nd Lowland Volunteers.

213. Pitreavie, Fife The principal maritime command centre in Scotland, housed in a large bunker 120 feet below the trim lawns of Pitreavie Castle. In peacetime Pitreavie is the location of HQ Northern Maritime Air Region (NORMAR), RAF, and the RN's Flag Officer Scotland and Northern Ireland (FOSNI). These commanders are subordinate to HQ 18 (Maritime) Group RAF Strike Command and Commander-in-Chief Fleet (CINCFLEET) in the automated Joint Maritime HQ bunker at Northwood, London. When the NATO chain of command is activated, these British national commands become NATO ones in charge of forces assigned to the Supreme Allied Commander Atlantic (SACLANT), an American admiral based at Norfolk, Virginia. CINCFLEET at Northwood becomes Commander-in-Chief Channel (CINCHAN) and Commander-in-Chief Eastern Atlantic (CINCEASTLANT). Simultaneously, Pitreavie's naval component would become Commander North Atlantic (COMNORLANT) and Commander North East Channel (COMNORECHAN), while its RAF component would become Commander Air North Atlantic (COMMAIRNORLANT) and Commander Air North Channel (COMMAIRNORCHAN).

All this means that Pitreavie exercises control of NATO air and surface fleet forces from the North Sea to the North Pole, as directed by Northwood. Maritime air forces under Pitreavie's control consist of not only the RAF Nimrod, US/NATO P-3 and NATO Atlantic LRMPAS in the area but also maritime strike RAF Buccaneers (and probably USAF F-111s) and two RAF Phantom fighter squadrons (one at Leuchars, one at Coningsby) which are assigned to SACLANT.

There are two units concerned with the staffing of Pitreavie in wartime. Firstly, the Joint Maritime Operational Training Staff (JMOTS), normally based at Turnhouse, goes to Pitreavie during major maritime exercises (such as the JMC series) and would be at Pitreavie during a war. Secondly, an RAF Auxiliary unit, known as 2 Maritime HQ, supports HQ NORMAR and has Pitreavie as a training and wartime base. The unit monitors potentially hostile ships and submarines in peacetime and would operate with and direct Nimrods in wartime. It is one of three such units in the UK. The RNR also has an HQ unit at Pitreavie.

Pitreavie has a 'reserve button for Polaris'.[113] It could initiate the relay of launch orders to British SSBNs on behalf of the RN Flag Officer Submarines once his bunker, also at Northwood, had been vaporised. However, such a relay would require that the VLF radio transmitters needed to reach submerged submarines remained intact or that SSBNs adopt the unlikely practice of coming near enough to the surface in patrol areas to receive orders using LF radio.

In the public mind Pitreavie is more familiar as a main Meteorological Office and as the Northern Rescue Co-ordination Centre. To journalists it is well known as the office of the RN and RAF PROs for Scotland. As one may gather, these functions are subsidiary to those of the main military commands described above.

Various writers have described Pitreavie's role as a surveillance centre concerned mainly with Soviet naval vessels and submarines.[114] Accordingly, it seems likely that this base receives surveillance data directly or derived from OSIS via the FOSIC in London and in particular, data from undersea sensors in Northern Waters. Pitreavie co-ordinates maritime surveillance operations in its designated territory of some 1.75 million square miles. On the basis of intelligence derived from the various sources it allocates tasks to the RAF's Nimrod force at Kinloss; aircraft can be directed to specific ocean areas to localise Soviet submarines. Pitreavie also co-ordinates surveillance with US, Canadian, West German, Dutch, French and Norwegian LRMPAS, presumably in concert with other Maritime

HQS at Bodø (Norway) and Keflavik (Iceland) and command centres elsewhere.

Besides overt military operations Pitreavie supervises 'Operation Hornbeam', in which some Scottish trawler skippers log Soviet ship sightings during fishing expeditions in Northern Waters and report their findings on a special radio frequency to the Joint Intelligence Section at Pitreavie. Campbell has stated that larger trawlers, such as the *Gaul*, which disappeared in 1976, may sometimes carry naval intelligence officers.[115] There are rumours that 'Hornbeam' extends to lighthouse keepers and customs officers who may occasionally make contact with Soviet commercial vessels.

To fulfil its roles, Pitreavie requires extensive communications facilities. Some 120 personnel work at Pitreavie, many of them responsible for telecommunications. Communications sites connected with Pitreavie include not only the HF transmitter/receiver site overlooking the north end of the Forth Road Bridge, but also Balado Bridge, Crimond, Milltown and probably Knock Hill. Pitreavie is connected to the DCN by telephone/telex landline. As part of Project Uniter these links will be upgraded and interconnected with other systems. It is likely that Pitreavie has already received TARE and TASS equipment as part of the NATO Integrated Communications System (NICS, see pp. 118–19), installed 'in the latest underground communications block.'[116] Further integration into NICS will occur when Pitreavie is linked by microwave to the new relay station on Cullaloe Hill. This will not only give commanders here direct access to the NATO satellite communications system via Balado Bridge, but will also enable them to use the BT 'Backbone' microwave system, e.g. for receipt of radar pictures of the command area transmitted from UKADGE radar stations. The Cullaloe link will also integrate Pitreavie with the UK joint services microwave system, BOXER.

As emphasis on the military significance of the north-east Atlantic grows, Pitreavie will assume increasing importance as one of the UK's main command centres.

214. Rosyth, Fife   The only major UK base for RN surface ships outside the south of England. There are two major facilities here – the naval base and the naval dockyard.

The naval base is known as HMS *Cochrane* and consists of the following:

(a) The Fleet Accommodation Centre for crews of vessels under the control of the Flag Officer Scotland and Northern Ireland. There are over 1,250 RN personnel here. The centre was built in 1968 and is also responsible for providing some aspects of training to RN personnel in junior management positions.

(b) HQ Mine Counter-measures Flotilla, consisting of the 1st, 3rd and 10th Mine Counter-measures Squadrons. These operate a mix of minesweepers and minehunters.

(c) HQ Fishery Protection Squadron. This is responsible not only for patrolling UK fishing grounds but also for security of offshore oil and gas installations. It has nine 'Ton' class minesweepers, five 'Island' and two 'Castle' class offshore patrol vessels.

(d) The 6th Frigate Squadron, consisting of up to eight Type 12 'Rothesay' class frigates, assigned to NATO force escort, with a primary role of anti-submarine warfare. In 1985 it will be joined at Rosyth by a new squadron operating four Type 42 destroyers.[117]

(e) HMS *Caledonia*, which is an RN Engineering School for training artificers. About 600 apprentices are here at any one time. This facility is to close and transfer to Gosport in 1985. The buildings will then become part of the Fleet Accommodation Centre.

(f) Fleet Maintenance Group, which operates three floating dry docks.

HMS *Cochrane* also controls a Marine Services School (training RMAS seamen), a Salvage Depot and the Joint Maritime Operational Training Staff at Turnhouse and Pitreavie. Further details of these and other units at Rosyth can be found elsewhere.[118]

The naval dockyard at Rosyth is now destined to become even more important due to the closure of Chatham and some changes at Devonport. Rosyth was selected in 1963 as the first dockyard for nuclear submarine refits. Its primary work is the major refitting of the UK's four SSBNs but following the closure of Chatham, Rosyth will also refit the RN's SSNs from 1984. The dockyard is theoretically capable of refitting any of the RN's ships, but apart from nuclear submarine work the yard is chiefly concerned with locally-based minesweepers and offshore patrol vessels.

The SSBN refits, which were costing £96 million a time in 1982, are carried out every three and a half years on each of the four submarines, and take 18 months to complete. They are dovetailed so that there is always one SSBN under refit. The refit involves removal of the nuclear reactor core, X-raying of welds and overhaul of the hull and all systems. Radioactive waste from the de-fuelling of the reactor is stored in barges, moved ashore then taken by special train to BNFL's Windscale reprocessing plant. These waste trains will undoubtedly become more frequent as the SSN refit work at Rosyth builds up.

Apart from the problem of radioactive waste disposal, there have been serious concerns about the safety of people working on nuclear propulsion systems at Rosyth dockyard. Medical tests in 1980 revealed that all 197 of a sample of workers in the nuclear section of the yard had a form of chromosome aberration associated with long-term cumulative radiation exposure. The MOD subsequently refused to release the medical inspection records of yard workers to the TGWU.

In March 1981 a cobalt isotope used for monitoring equipment disappeared. Its protective case was found a few weeks later, but the 3 inch isotope itself was not found until late January 1982, in the Polaris refit dock which had been searched many times before. It is likely that this was an attempt to draw attention to lax security and safety standards in the yard. Surprisingly, at such a potentially lethal workplace, cheap alcohol is sold at several bars in the yard. In 1981 a worker who had been drinking was overcome by fumes and died, as did two of his workmates in a rescue bid. Working practices appear to leave much to be desired. One full-time union official said, 'there are working practices and dockyard practices . . . don't ask me what goes on. I'm only told what my shop stewards decide to tell me, and don't name me, it would create more trouble.'[119]

In April 1983 further problems were created when the first RN SSN to be de-commissioned, HMS *Dreadnought*, was towed into Rosyth to allow its radioactivity to decay. While the US navy is sinking its obsolete nuclear submarine hulls in the Atlantic, the Royal Navy has been unable to reach a decision on how to dispose of these radiating hulks. Fears amongst the workforce that the RN's 'solution' would be to dump more of these vessels at Rosyth prompted 1,500 electricians and shipwrights in the yard to black any work on *Dreadnought*. Their concern is unlikely to diminish following revelations that the 'Swiftsure' class SSNs have serious weld faults in the reactor cooling system.

Also at Rosyth is a submarine pressure testing facility. Work was started on this by Taylor Woodrow in the 1970s, but the pressure vessel failed at half its design pressure in 1978. Taylor Woodrow were then awarded a new contract for £10 million in 1981. There are likely to be other contracts issued for modifications to the dockyard for refitting Trident submarines.

Other units at Rosyth include an outstation of the Fleet and Dockyard Support Division of AMTE, which provides scientific personnel and equipment support to the base and dockyard, the Northern Area HQ of the MOD police, the Naval Provost Service and Naval Clearance Diving Teams for Scotland and Northern Ireland and, it is believed, one of the four Naval Emergency Monitoring Teams in the UK (see *Faslane*).

Rosyth is the largest employer in Fife, with over 6,000 employed in the dockyard by the end of 1983 and around 2,000 elsewhere on the base. In contrast to the overall reduction in MOD civilian jobs, expansion at Rosyth will create 600 more posts there over the period 1981–85. Strong vested interests in this scale of employment, a great deal of it in skilled trades, makes it difficult to gain ground in arguments for conversion of military industries to socially useful production, but Fife Trades Council was making some progress with this in 1983.

A women's peace camp was set up at Rosyth early in 1983.

215. St Andrews, Fife   TAVR centre, a platoon of 15 (Scottish Volunteers) Battalion, The Parachute Regiment, and a detachment of Tayforth Universities OTC.

216. Shanwell, Tayport, Fife MOD (Air) Upper Atmosphere Centre, one of only three Met. Office stations in Scotland with radiosonde facilities. Closely involved in upper atmosphere forecasting for operations by military aircraft and missiles and as part of the fall-out warning chain.

217. Stirling Stirling Castle is the Regimental HQ of an infantry regiment, but has only ceremonial functions. TAVR units in the town are a detachment of Tayforth Universities OTC and E Company, 1st Battalion 51st Highland Volunteers.

218. Stirling (Drip Bridge) Army training camp, used by a variety of units. A detachment of 324 Engineer Park is based here.

219. Turnhouse (Edinburgh Airport) Two military facilities are located here:

(a) An RAF station under 18 (Maritime) Group, RAF Strike Command. Base of the 25 personnel of the Joint Maritime Operational Training Staff (JMOTS), an RN/RAF unit which plans and directs the three or four Joint Maritime Course (JMC) NATO exercises held in the North Sea and north-east Atlantic each year. JMOTS moves from Turnhouse to the Maritime HQ at Pitreavie during these exercises.

Turnhouse receives regular visits from NATO maritime aircraft in connection with JMOTS and Pitreavie. It is also the base of a University Air Squadron which gives basic flying training to prospective RAF aircrew studying at the two local universities, an Air Experience Flight for Air Cadets, and an RAF Devon for light transport duties between the RAF bases under the command of the Air Officer Commanding Scotland and Northern Ireland at Pitreavie. Some personnel from Pitreavie are also housed at Turnhouse.

(b) The HQ 24 Group ROC, controlling the UKWMO's nuclear blast and fall-out monitoring posts in East Central Scotland and the Borders.

Notes

1. The strategists' Scotland

1. Tom Gervasi, *Arsenal of Democracy II: American Military Power in the 1980s and the Origins of the New Cold War,* New York: Grove Press 1981, p.5.
2. See, for example, Dan Smith, *Non-nuclear Military Options for Britain,* Peace Studies Papers No. 6, School of Peace Studies, University of Bradford and London: Housmans 1982, and *Defence without the Bomb: The Report of the Alternative Defence Commission,* London: Taylor and Francis 1983.
3. See Duncan Campbell, *War Plan UK: The Truth about Civil Defence in Britain*, London: Burnett Books 1982, chapter 6.
4. For example Geoffrey Pattie MP, Parliamentary Under-Secretary of State for Defence for the RAF, speech to the Air League, quoted in *Air Pictorial*, vol. 43 no. 3, March 1981, pp.102, 110; John Lehman, US Secretary of the Navy, in 'Lehman seeks superiority', *International Defense Review*, vol.15 no.5, 1982, p.547, and John Nott, interviewed in *International Defense Review,* vol.14 no.12, 1981, p.1,570.
5. *SECNAV/CNO Report, Fiscal Year 1983,* Washington DC: Navy Internal Relations Activity, Office of the Chief of Information 1982, pp.6,7.
6. Quoted in *The Guardian*, 14 April 1982.
7. Michael MccGwire, *Power At Sea II: Superpowers and Navies,* Adelphi Paper No.123, London: International Insititute for Strategic Studies 1976, p.18. The US Chief of Naval Operations has stated that 'our plan would be as the first line of defense to strike . . . the submarine bases from which the nuclear powered submarines operate.' (US Congress, Senate Committee on Armed Services, *Fiscal Year 1979 Authorization for Military Procurement,* Part 5, Washington DC: US Government Printing Office 1978, p.4,321.)
8. Michael MccGwire, 'The Tomahawk and general purpose naval forces', in Richard K. Betts (ed.), *Cruise Missiles: Technology, Strategy, Politics,* Washington DC: The Brookings Institution 1981, p.251; Peter Whiteley, 'Military operations on the Northern Flank', in Lars B. Wallin (ed.), *The Northern Flank in a Central European War,* Stockholm: Swedish National Defence Research Institute 1982, p.151.

9. North Atlantic Assembly, *Report on the Activities of the Joint Sub-committee on the Northern Region,* Report No. W 139 MC-PC/NR(79)4, Brussels: North Atlantic Assembly International Secretariat 1979, p.10. See also US Congress, House Committee on Foreign Affairs, *Northern European Security Issues: Report of a Staff Study Mission to Five NATO Countries and Sweden,* Washington DC: US Government Printing Office 1983, pp.2–3, 7.

10. Caspar W. Weinberger, *Annual Report to the Congress, Fiscal Year 1984,* Washington DC: US Government Printing Office 1983, p.235.

11. David A. Rosenberg, 'The origins of overkill: nuclear weapons and American strategy, 1945–1960', *International Security,* vol.7 no.4, Spring 1983, p.43; *Washington Post,* 21 May 1983.

12. For further discussion of the dangers of inadvertent nuclear war in this region see Barry R. Posen, 'Inadvertent nuclear war? Escalation and NATO's Northern Flank', *International Security,* vol.7 no.2, Fall 1982, pp.28–54.

13. See for example US Congress, House Committee on Foreign Affairs and Senate Committee on Foreign Relations, *Fiscal Year 1982 Arms Control Impact Statements,* Washington DC: US Government Printing Office 1981, p.372.

14. *New York Times,* 19 May 1983.

15. House of Commons Defence Committee, *Strategic Nuclear Weapons Policy,* Fourth Report, Session 1980–81, HC 36, London: HMSO 1981, p.80.

16. US Congress, House Appropriations Committee, *Department of Defense Appropriations for 1983,* Part 4, Washington DC: US Government Printing Office 1982, p.553.

17. *Tactical and Strategic Anti-submarine Warfare: A SIPRI Monograph,* Stockholm: Almqvist and Wiksell/MIT Press 1974, p.80; *World Armaments and Disarmament: SIPRI Yearbook 1979,* London: Taylor and Francis 1979, p.433.

18. US Congress, House Committee on Foreign Affairs and Senate Committee on Foreign Relations, *op. cit.* p.355.

19. *World Armaments and Disarmament: SIPRI Yearbook 1979, op. cit.* pp.440–41.

20. US Congress, House Committee on International Relations and Senate Committee on Foreign Relations, *Fiscal Year 1979 Arms Control Impact Statements,* Washington DC: US Government Printing Office 1978, pp.166, 185–86.

21. Caspar W. Weinberger, *Annual Report to the Congress, Fiscal Year 1984,* Washington DC: US Government Printing Office 1983, p. 209.

22. *Defence in the 1980s: Statement on the Defence Estimates 1980,* vol.1, Cmnd.7826–I, London: HMSO 1980, p.32.

23. *Navy International,* vol.87 no.3, March 1982, p.907.

24. *ibid.*

25. House of Commons Defence Committee, *Statement on the Defence*

Estimates 1981, Second Report, Session 1980–81, HC 302, London: HMSO 1981, pp.57–58.

26. Nils Ørvik, 'NATO and the Northern Rim', *NATO Review*, no.2, April 1980, p.14; *South East Air Review*, November 1977, p.244; North Atlantic Assembly, *op. cit.* p.21.

27. Air Commodore George Chesworth, Director of Quartering, MOD(Air), quoted in *The Stornoway Gazette*, 15 December 1979.

28. Rogers' arguments are set out by him in 'Enhancing deterrence – raising the nuclear threshold', *NATO Review*, vol.30 no.6, 1983, pp.6–9, and 'Sword and shield: ACE attack of Warsaw Pact follow-on forces', *NATO's Sixteen Nations*, vol.28 no.1, February–March 1983, pp.16–26. They are put in rather a different perspective in US Congress, House Appropriations Committee, *Department of Defense Appropriations for 1983*, Part 4, Washington DC: US Government Printing Office 1982, pp.424–25; *Aviation Week and Space Technology*, vol.113 no.1, 7 July 1980, p.48, and vol.117 no.18, 1 November 1982, p.77; and Rik Coolsaet, 'US changes rules of war', *END Journal*, issue 4, June–July 1983, pp.22–23.

29. Ronald T. Pretty (ed.), *Jane's Weapon Systems 1981–82*, London: Jane's 1981, pp.232–33; Paul Claesson, *Grønland Middelhavets Perle: et Indblik i Amerikansk Atomkrigs-Forberedelse*, Copenhagen: Eirene 1983, pp.71–78.

30. For a fuller description of NACCS see Michael Feazel, 'NATO plans to fund air control studies', *Aviation Week and Space Technology*, vol.118 no.2, 10 January 1983. pp.79–87, and *NATO's Fifteen Nations*, Special Issue 2/80.

31. For further details of NAEGIS See Michael Wilson, 'NATO launches NADGE enhancement production phase', *Jane's Defence Review*, vol.4 no.1, 1983, pp.83–84.

32. *Flight International*, 16 October 1982, p.1,103.

33. Wing Commander P. Burton, RAF, 'AEW', *Air Pictorial*, vol.43 no.9, September 1981, p.341.

34. 'B52/Harpoon changes set', *Aviation Week and Space Technology*, vol.117 no.7, 16 August 1982, p.25.

35. Owen Wilkes and Nils P. Gleditsch, *Onkel Sams Kaniner: Teknisk Etterretning i Norge*, Oslo: Pax Forlag 1981, chapter 5; Owen Wilkes and Nils P. Gleditsch, *Intelligence Installations in Norway: Their Number, Location, Function and Legality*, PRIO publication s-4/79, Oslo: International Peace Research Institute 1979, pp.59–63.

36. Derek Wood, 'Re-shaping the Royal Air Force', *International Defense Review*, vol.15 no.3, 1982, p.315.

2. Military expansion in perspective

1. *Statement on the Defence Estimates 1982*, vol.2, Cmnd.8529–II, London: HMSO 1982, p.57.

2. North Atlantic Assembly, *Report on the Activities of the Joint Sub-Committee on the Northern Region,* Report No. w 139 mc-pc/nr(79)4, Brussels: 1979, p.21.
3. Derek Wood, *Attack Warning Red,* London: Macdonald and Jane's 1976, p.275.
4. *Stornoway Gazette,* 23 September, 21 October and 2 December 1960.
5. *The Scotsman,* 20 December 1957.
6. *Stornoway Gazette,* 17 May 1980.
7. Keith Simpson, Directorate of Works (Air), Property Services Agency, oral evidence to Stornoway Public Inquiry, 17 March 1981.
8. *Sunday Standard,* 29 August 1982.
9. Duncan Campbell, *War Plan uk: The Truth about Civil Defence in Britain,* London: Burnett Books 1982, p.184.

3. The armed society: the impact of the military in Scotland

1. Moray District Council, *Forres Area Local Plan: Survey Report,* Elgin 1979, p.3.
2. David Greenwood and John Short, *Military Installations and Local Economies – a Case Study: the Moray Air Stations,* Aberdeen Studies in Defence Economics No.4, Aberdeen: Centre for Defence Studies 1973, p.12.
3. *ibid.* p.13.
4. *Statement on the Defence Estimates 1982,* vol.1, Cmnd.8529–1,London: hmso 1982, p.38.
5. *Navy News,* October 1982, p.4; *The Scotsman,* 11 February 1982.
6. Harry W. Richardson, *Elements of Regional Economics,* Harmondsworth: Penguin 1969, p.32; see also Greenwood and Short, *op. cit.* and Timothy Stone, *Analysing the Regional Aspect of Defence Spending: a Survey,* Aberdeen Studies in Defence Economics No.3, Aberdeen: Centre for Defence Studies 1973.
7. *The Sunday Standard,* 29 August 1982.
8. *Statement on the Defence Estimates 1982,* vol.2, Cmnd. 8529–II, London: hmso 1982, p.57.
9. *Press and Journal,* 24 December 1979.
10. Examples of this in Lewis and the Uists are given in Comhairle nan Eilean, Development Services Committee, Report by Director of Planning and Development on Application No.A/79/602, Stornoway 1979, p.1/15; *Oban Times,* 19 November 1981; *West Highland Free Press,* 10 August 1979; Philippa Simpson, 'The Royal Artillery guided weapons range (Hebrides) – its social and economic impact on the Uists', unpublished diploma thesis, Department of Town and Regional Planning, University of Glasgow 1979, pp.79–80.
11. Allen Garry, 'Class struggle in the Highlands?', *Cran Tara,* no.15,

Autumn 1981, p.12. The figure relates to estates over 2,000 acres.

12. *Press and Journal*, 27 October 1979.

13. National Air Traffic Services, *United Kingdom NOTAM*, No.B12/1982, January 1982.

14. *Press and Journal*, 12 November 1977.

15. Colin Strong and Duff Hart-Davis, *Fighter Pilot*, London: Queen Anne Press/BBC 1981, p.150.

16. *Press and Journal*, 14 August 1981.

17. James Wellbeloved MP, Parliamentary Under-Secretary of State for Defence for the RAF, letter to Russell Johnston MP, 21 March 1979; Group Captain John Neville RAF, statement to public meeting on low-flying, Huntly, 12 February 1980; John Dalling, 'Price of peace', *RAF News*, no.538, 16 December 1981–12 January 1982, p.9.

18. Robert Prest, *F4 Phantom: A Pilot's Story*, London: Corgi 1981, p.240.

19. *Flight International*, 26 August 1978, p.627.

20. *The Guardian*, 15 September 1982.

21. *Press and Journal*, 2 September 1982.

22. Scottish Office, 'Report on local planning inquiry', June 1981.

23. T. Miller, 'Military airfields and rural planning', *Town Planning Review*, vol.44 no.1, January 1973, p.32.

24. *The Guardian*, 29 April 1982.

25. *The Scottish Highlands and Islands: On the Water*, Highlands and Islands Development Board tourist brochure, 1982.

26. Highland Regional Council, *North-West Sutherland Local Plan*, Inverness 1980, para.4.3.5.

27. *Sanity*, October 1982, p.14.

28. *The Sunday Standard*, 29 August 1982.

29. *Press and Journal*, 31 July 1978.

4. Directory of bases

1. The Right Hon. Lord Nugent (Chairman), *Report of the Defence Lands Committee 1971–73*, London: HMSO 1973, p.431.

2. *RAF News*, no.554, 8–21 September 1982, pp.12–13.

3. Duncan Campbell, 'A military peep over the North Sea horizon?', *New Scientist*, 6 March 1975, pp.563–64; *Sunday Telegraph*, 19 October 1975.

4. Nils Ørvik, 'NATO and the Northern Rim', *NATO Review*, no.2, April 1980, p.14.

5. Anon., 'Keeping the Bear at bay', *Royal Air Force Yearbook 1982*, p.25.

6. Michael J Gething, 'Elder Forest '80', *Defence*, vol.11 no.6, June 1980, p.478.

7. Derek Wood, 'Re-shaping the Royal Air Force', *International Defense Review*, vol.15 no.3, 1982, p.315.

8. *Press and Journal*, 10 April 1981.

9. Ian Walker, 'The boys on the base', *Observer Magazine*, 6 March 1983, p.11.

10. R. J. Raggett (ed.), *Jane's Military Communications 1981*, London: Jane's 1981, p.572.

11. Desmond Ball, *Can Nuclear War Be Controlled?*, Adelphi Paper No.169, London: International Institute for Strategic Studies 1981, p.22.

12. Ronald T. Pretty (ed.), *Jane's Weapon Systems 1977*, London: Jane's 1977, p.206.

13. Desmond Ball, *op.cit.* p.25.

14. US Congress, House Appropriations Committee, *Military Construction Appropriations for 1981*, Part 1, p.1,523.

15. *Nuclear Weapons Data File*, London: Aviation Studies Atlantic (no date) Section 2, p.8.

16. Anon., 'Air force modernizing command, control units', *Aviation Week and Space Technology*, vol.116 no.23, 7 June 1982, p.81.

17. Duncan Campbell and Linda Melvern, 'America's big ear on Europe', *New Statesman*, 18 July 1980, pp.10–14.

18. R. Harris and J. Paxman, *A Higher Form of Killing: The Secret Story of Gas and Germ Warfare*, London: Chatto and Windus 1982.

19. The Right Hon. Lord Nugent, *op.cit.* p.379.

20. *AMTE: Admiralty Marine Technology Establishment*, London: HMSO 1980, p.13.

21. *Press and Journal*, 4 September 1981.

22. *West Highland Free Press*, 20 October 1978.

23. Anon., 'Breakthrough in single-seat night attack?' *International Defense Review*, vol.15 no.7, 1982, p.832.

24. Clarence A. Robinson, 'Antiship missiles studied to block sea chokepoints', *Aviation Week and Space Technology*, vol.118 no.9, 28 February 1983, pp.24–26.

25. Michael MccGwire, 'The Tomahawk and general purpose naval forces', in Richard K. Betts (ed.), *Cruise Missiles: Technology, Strategy, Politics*, Washington DC: The Brookings Institution 1981, p.242.

26. *ibid.* p.251.

27. *The Scotsman*, 19 May 1982.

28. *International Defense Review*, vol.5 no.4, August 1972, p.363.

29. U. Bruhns, 'Tactical communications navy', *NATO's Fifteen Nations*, Special Issue no.2, 1980. p.60.

30. The Right Hon. Lord Nugent, *op.cit.* p.357.

31. *The Scotsman*, 1 February 1980.

32. *The Shetland Times*, 17 April 1981.

33. *Statement on the Defence Estimates 1981*, vol.1, Cmnd.8212–I, London: HMSO 1981, p.27.

34. Commentator at RAF Leuchars Open Day, 4 September 1982; *RAF News*, no.554, 8–21 September 1982, p.13.

35. Duncan Campbell, *Phonetappers and the Security State*, London: New Statesman Report 2, 1981.

36. Peter Laurie, *Beneath the City Streets,* London: Granada 1979, chapter 7.
37. *The Scotsman Magazine,* no.12, March 1981, p.23.
38. Duncan Campbell, *op.cit.*
39. *us Naval Security Group Activity Edzell: Introductory Public Relations Booklet,* London: us Navy 1976.
40. *ibid.*
41. us Congress, House Appropriations Committee, *Military Construction Appropriations for 1981,* Part 1, p.1,124.
42. *World Armaments and Disarmament: sipri Yearbook 1979,* London: Taylor and Francis 1979, pp.277–78.
43. us Congress, House Appropriations Committee, *Military Construction Appropriations for 1983,* Part 3, p.1,255.
44. *Armed Forces,* December 1982, p.407.
45. John W. R. Taylor (ed.), *Jane's All the World's Aircraft 1980–81,* London: Jane's 1980, p.237.
46. *Press and Journal,* 10 December 1981.
47. *Statement on the Defence Estimates 1980,* vol.1, Cmnd.7826–I, London: hmso 1980, p.37.
48. Colin Tredwell, 'Lossie moves to big league', *raf News,* no.573,20 May–3 June 1983, p.12.
49. *ibid.*
50. Peter Laurie, *op.cit.* p.170.
51. *rusi and Brassey's Annual 1975–76,* p.386.
52. *Aviation Week and Space Technology,* vol.118 no.19, 9 May 1983, p.71.
53. *The Sunday Standard,* 14 February 1982.
54. R. J. Raggett (ed.), *Jane's Military Communications 1981,* London: Jane's 1981, p.578.
55. L. Rohrholt, 'Satellite communications', *nato's Fifteen Nations,* Special Issue no.2, 1980, p.80.
56. *Press and Journal,* 8 December 1979.
57. Mark Hewish, 'uk Torpedo Programs: an update', *International Defense Review,* vol. 14 no.6, 1981, p.786.
58. *Report of the Study Group on the Status of Royal Ordnance Factories,* sgs/rof Consultative Document, Defence Open Government Document No.81/28, London: Ministry of Defence 1981, Annex B, Appendix III, Sheet 1.
59. *World Armaments and Disarmament: sipri Yearbook 1982,* London: Taylor and Francis 1982, p.281. Frank Barnaby, writing in *The Guardian,* 2 December 1982, put the figure at 23,000.
60. Duncan Campbell, 'Dangers of the nuclear convoys', *New Statesman,* vol.101 no.2,612, 10 April 1981, pp.6–8.
61. *The Scotsman,* 10 March 1981.
62. us Congress, House Appropriations Committee, *Military Construction Appropriations for 1982,* p.446.
63. Peter Blaker mp, Minister of State for the Armed Forces, letter to John

Mackay MP 31 July 1981.

64. *Underwater Engineering Directory 1973–74,* London: Spearhead Publications 1973, pp.129–30.

65. The Right Hon. Lord Nugent, *op.cit.* p.371.

66. *ibid.* p.361.

67. Terry Gander, *Encyclopaedia of the Modern British Army,* Cambridge: Patrick Stephens 1982, p.66.

68. INM: *Institute of Naval Medicine,* London: HMSO 1981, p.15.

69. *The Scotsman,* 7 May 1960.

70. US Congress, House Appropriations Committee, *Military Construction Appropriations for 1980,* Part 5, p.907.

71. US Congress, House Appropriations Committee, *Department of Defense Appropriations for 1983,* Part 7, p.507.

72. *Underwater Engineering Directory 1973–74,* London: Spearhead Publications 1973, p.129.

73. John Moore (ed.), *Jane's Fighting Ships 1980–81,* London: Jane's 1980, p.680.

74. *New Statesman,* vol.102 no.2,646, 4 December 1981.

75. Personal communication, 1982.

76. John Moore (ed.), *Jane's Fighting Ships 1976–77,* London: Jane's 1976, p.641.

77. Russell Warren Howe, *Weapons,* London: Abacus 1980, p.51.

78. *Aviation Week and Space Technology,* vol.113 no.1, 7 July 1980, p.48.

79. *The Scotsman,* 7 December 1981.

80. US Congress, House Appropriations Committee, *Military Construction Appropriations for 1979,* Part 2, p.250.

81. Personal communication, February 1983.

82. Office of the Assistant Secretary of Defense (Public Affairs), *Fiscal Year 1984 Military Construction Program,* News Release No.40/83, Washington DC, 10 February 1983, p.52.

83. DPEE: *Directorate of Proof and Experimental Establishments,* London: HMSO 1982.

84. *Underwater Engineering Directory 1973–74,* London: Spearhead Publications 1973, pp.129–30.

85. Derek Wood, 'Re-shaping the Royal Air Force', *International Defense Review,* vol. 15 no.3, 1982, p.316.

86. See Caspar W. Weinberger, *Annual Report to the Congress Fiscal Year 1984,* Washington DC: US Government Printing Office 1983, p.235.

87. SIPRI *Yearbook of World Armaments and Disarmament 1969–70,* Stockholm: Almqvist and Wiksell 1970, p.117.

88. Cited in William Arkin, 'Nuclear weapons in Europe', in Mary Kaldor and Dan Smith (eds), *Disarming Europe,* London: Merlin 1982, p.54.

89. *The Scotsman,* 6 October 1980.

90. Ben J. Ullings, 'MLD's Orions at Valkenburg', *Armed Forces,* November 1982, p.395.

91. Ronald T. Pretty (ed.), *Jane's Weapon Systems 1980–81,* London: Jane's 1980, p.135.

92. *Defense Week*, vol.4 no.15, 14 March 1983, p.2.

93. Ben J. Ullings, *op.cit.* p.394.

94. Anon., 'New aircraft will reshape Royal Air Force deployment', *Flight International*, 5 September 1981.

95. *The Scotsman*, 26 May 1982.

96. *Report of the Study Group on the Status of Royal Ordnance Factories*, SGS/ROF Consultative Document, Defence Open Government Document No.81/28, London: Ministry of Defence 1981, Annex B, Appendix III, Sheet 2.

97. The Right Hon. Lord Nugent, *op.cit.* p.363.

98. US Congress, House Appropriations Committee, *Military Construction Appropriations for 1984*, Part 2, pp.733–35.

99. *RAE: Royal Aircraft Establishment*, London: HMSO p.38.

100. *The Scotsman*, 1 March 1979.

101. *Statement on the Defence Estimates 1981*, vol.1, Cmnd.8212–I, London: HMSO 1981, p.51.

102. Peter Laurie, *Beneath the City Streets*, London: Granada 1979, p.162.

103. E.A. Chris Wren, 'The part-timers', *Royal Air Force Yearbook 1977*, p.48.

104. Terry Gander, *Encyclopaedia of the Modern British Army*, Cambridge: Patrick Stephens 1982, p.66.

105. Duncan Campbell, 'American bases in Britain', in *Britain and the Bomb*, London: New Statesman Report 3, 1981, p.44.

106. James Bamford, *The Puzzle Palace*, London: Sidgwick and Jackson 1983, p.xiii.

107. *New Statesman*, 2 February 1979, p.7.

108. *New Statesman*, 16 May 1980, pp.738–44, and 23 May 1980, p.774–77.

109. Duncan Campbell and Mark Hosenball, in *Time Out*, 21 May 1976, and *Undercurrents*, no.24, October–November 1977, pp.20–23.

110. *ASWE: Admiralty Surface Weapons Establishment*, London: HMSO 1982.

111. Paul S. Mercer, *A Directory of British Military Aviation and US Military Aviation in Europe*, Loughborough: Jackson Publications 1981, p.11; commentator at RAF Leuchars open day, 4 September 1982.

112. Mark Hewish, 'Sharpening Rapier for the 1990s', *International Defense Review*, vol.15 no.12, 1982, p.1,704.

113. Duncan Campbell, 'The British bomb part III', *New Statesman*, 1 May 1981, p.9.

114. Tom Mangold, 'Cold war under the sea', *The Listener*, 13 October 1977.

115. *New Statesman*, 2 February 1979.

116. William Robertson, 'Rockets galore', *The Sunday Standard*, 7 June 1981.

117. *The Scotsman*, 27 August 1983.

118. Paul Beaver, *Encyclopaedia of the Modern Royal Navy*, Cambridge: Patrick Stephens 1982; *The Navy List*, London: HMSO annual.

119. *The Sunday Standard*, 8 November 1981.

Index

Fortress Scotland gives the facts on Scotland's military build-up. Knowing the facts is not enough. Put them to use.

Contact Scottish CND, 420 Sauchiehall Street, Glasgow G2 3JD. Telephone: 041 331 2878. Enclose your name, address & telephone no. with all correspondence. Rates for one year's membership are:

Adult	£6
Household	£9
Youth/Unwaged	£2
Student	£3

If paying by banker's order (forms available at your bank), make the order payable to: The Co-operative Bank PLC, 147 Buchanan Street, Glasgow G1 2RG, bank code 83-91-25, for the account of the Scottish Campaign for Nuclear Disarmament, Account No. 50087934.

Alice Cook and Gwyn Kirk

Greenham Women Everywhere

Dreams, ideas and actions from the women's peace movement

The first women's peace camp was set up in September 1981 at
Greenham Common. It has been a major catalyst in the growth of
opposition, both in the UK and abroad, to the escalation of the
nuclear arms race. **Greenham Women Everywhere** describes the
dreams, nightmares and personal statements of some of the many
women who, faced with the nuclear threat, have made the difficult
transition from private anxiety to collective commitment. It shows
their determination, imagination and strength; it discusses the
response of the media and the importance of legal support; it asserts
a belief in non-violent direct action which has inspired a campaign
well beyond Greenham.

Greenham Women Everywhere is a book to be read by activists in
the peace movement, by feminists, and by all those concerned about
the urgent need for nuclear disarmament.

0 86104 726 5   paperback   £3.50

Dan Smith and Ron Smith
The Economics of Militarism

Half a year's world military spending costs more than a ten-year
programme to meet basic food and health needs in poor countries.
This book explains how and why military spending occurs. It
examines the state interests which motivate it, the bureaucracies
which administer it and the corporations which profit from it.
The Economics of Militarism is a comprehensive introduction to the
consequences of arms spending which also investigates the economic
feasibility of disarmament.

0 86104 370 7   paperback   £2.95

Jerry W. Sanders

Peddlers of Crisis

The Committee on the Present Danger and the politics
of containment

Peddlers of Crisis reveals the influence of the US Committee on the
Present Danger, which shaped early cold war doctrine and now has
members in Reagan's administration.

'the best analysis of current US foreign policy that has been written
in recent years, of truly profound importance for scholars and
citizens alike' Richard Falk, Princeton University

'Sanders has struck gold; in fact, the historian's equivalent of
King Tut's tomb. Sanders has brought us a treasure of new insights
into the origins and aims of policies that *are* the present danger'
Daniel Ellsberg

'the scholarship is superior and the historical reporting is meticulous.
Nothing else available covers this important ground'
Richard Barnet, Insitute of Policy Studies (US)

0 86104 717 6   paperback   £5.95

Robert Aldridge
First Strike
The Pentagon's strategy for nuclear war

Robert Aldridge exposes the US military's bid for a first strike
capability and traces the logic of such a strategy to its deadly
conclusion.
First Strike examines each component of the arsenal — the Trident
submarine and missile, the MX missile, penetrating bombers and
cruise missiles. It strips away rationales for development to reveal
the corporate imperatives and aggressive intent of the current military
build-up.
Robert Aldridge is a former designer for Lockheed and author of
The Counterforce Syndrome.

0 86104 716 8   paperback   £5.95

Pluto books are available through your local bookshop. In case of
difficulty contact Pluto to find out local stockists or to obtain
catalogues/leaflets (Telephone 01-482 1973).
If all else fails write to:

   Pluto Press Limited
   Freepost (no stamp required)
   The Works
   105A, Torriano Avenue
   London NW5 1YP

To order, enclose a cheque/p.o. payable to Pluto Press to cover price
of book, plus 50p per book for postage and packing (£2.50
maximum).